GOD
&

GOD
&

Terrance A. Sweeney

WINSTON PRESS

Cover design: Terry Dugan

Copyright © 1985 by Terrance A. Sweeney.
All rights reserved. No part of this book may be reproduced in any
form without written permission from Winston Press, Inc.

Library of Congress Catalog Card Number: 83-60878

ISBN: 0-86683-804-X

Printed in the United States of America

5   4   3   2   1

Winston Press, Inc.
430 Oak Grove
Minneapolis, Minnesota 55403

To
Mary Melanson, Gerald Rozansky, M.D.,
and William Fulco, S.J.

*My thanks to
Gloria Landgraf and Sharon Gilbert
for their invaluable assistance
in preparing the manuscript,
and to
James A. Brown, Virginia Kelly,
George Horsfall and family*

CONTENTS

PREFACE

One year after being ordained a priest I found myself hating the One I prayed to and believed was God.

Nothing prepared me for my first year of priesthood—not growing up in a broken home with an absentee alcoholic father, not twelve years of Catholic education, nor an additional twelve of training as a Jesuit, nor graduate studies, nor the culture shock of living six weeks in the poorest countries of Latin America, nor working the terminal ward in a hospital, nor the burial of my father, who died alone in a skid row hotel. Nothing prepared me for what I was to experience that first year.

It was like being shocked awake by the terrifying winds of a hurricane—a tidal wave of humanity, with all its wild forces of suffering, hope, guilt, love, and despair. A penitent, burdened with guilt and anxiety over sex; an old woman, bitter and lonely, slowly dying in her one-room flat; a murderer finally confessing; a bride abused by her husband on their wedding night; a young man driven to insanity by his sick mother; a woman with two autistic childen begging me in the name of God to heal them—all of their personal, isolated traumas multiplied rapidly for me, and I began to feel as if I was standing beneath a towering, foreboding wall that was about to crash violently against the earth.

I wanted to stop the wave of suffering; and the faith of people and their expectations of me as priest and symbol of Jesus somehow told me this was possible. I began to feel like Jesus, who stood before the storm, stretched out his arm, and commanded: "Be still." The cry and anguish and misery of all those whose pain touched my life became the power of my command, and I stood like him before the tidal wave and ordered it in the name of love and compassion to STOP. The wave did not stop, nor the suffering, even, though I prayed from the depths of my heart. In June of 1974, the wave crashed on me with all its fury. I felt the violence and rage of humanity, and I found myself in a maelstrom of anger and tears shouting out to God and to my own soul: "I hate you!"

Call it what you will—God-shock, burnout, messiah complex, naive idealism—it happened. I felt as if I had been crushed and ravaged, limb by limb. And what was left were fragments of humanity and my identity strewn on some desolate wasteland called earth.

The months wore on, and, through exhaustion and confusion, the hatred subdued into a kind of nothingness. And still people came and asked me to hear their confessions, to anoint their dying fathers, to baptize their babies, to say Mass. But the difference was I no longer believed that God cared or healed. I no longer believed in God. I wanted to hide. I wanted to scream at the people: "Look at me, can't you see it in my eyes? Don't you feel it pouring out of me? God is dead, and I died with him, and your pain and joy and life don't touch me anymore!"

But I didn't scream, though I hid as best I could. I didn't tell them the painful truth, because I was afraid of scandalizing them and of being weak, broken, and helpless before the people who had exposed so much of their lives to me.

And then, for four years I went around asking people about *their* experiences of God, hoping somehow that in listening I could understand better the shattered fragments of my faith and identity, hoping to become someone new, something different from what I had experienced and believed in.

This book is a search for God, not the God of definitions and denominations, not the God of formulas or prayer rituals and preaching, but the God loved or rejected in the heart of human experience.

It helped me survive. In some way, I think it will help anyone who wonders about, desires, fights with, or loves God.

RAY BRADBURY

*One of the leading science fiction writers of our time,
Ray Bradbury has published over 300 stories and fourteen books. He wrote the screenplay for John Huston's
film version of Moby Dick. Ray's novel, Fahrenheit 451,
was made into a film by Francois Truffaut. He is a man
brimming with a remarkably joyful energy, which perhaps derives from his feeling of oneness with the
universe.*

SWEENEY: I try to base the interview on three fundamental
questions, and then if you want to change the questions or
modify them, fine; but the questions are: Who is God to you? How
has your relationship with God changed in your life? And, who
are you to God? Approach them any way you like.
BRADBURY: Very well, that's fascinating. I think we all, regardless
of religion, find we reach a certain point where religion becomes
boring, because of the way it is taught. I lecture one day a week;
the job of teaching day after day grinds a teacher down so that you
are not able to function as well as you should simply because
you've got to be good every day. It's impossible to do that. It's also
true for priests and for a minister or rabbi, with the many people
they have to see. So the whole thing gets covered with dust along
the way. Whether you're a teacher, lecturer, priest, or whatever,
you get discouraged at having to meet so many people, and trying
to do too much, and being a keeper of that many sheep. Then, too,
a lot of people are boring to start with. They never are good
teachers, they never are good priests or good ministers in the
sense of being able to build a verbal metaphor and deliver an
exciting message without being hypocritical, without oversell-
ing. So, I guess what happens along the way in the average church,

1

the average synagogue, is that a man who maybe isn't cut out to orate does a job of oration, puts people to sleep; so God gets lost somewhere between the priest and the people sitting there.

I grew up in a Baptist church, which was mainly a bore, and when you get older you envy the Catholic because there's more mystery, there's more drama, and you begin to understand how terrific a really good drama can be if it's acted out in a church or synagogue—the Jews have more fun at explaining the mystery and dramatizing it. The Greeks and the Romans had more fun originally with their gods and myths. So you get to a certain age, and you fall away and you say, "Well, I've had that, you know, I'll never come back to that." Which, of course, is ridiculous, as you've got to come back because you're faced with two mysteries constantly—the mystery of life and the mystery of death.

And so, as you get older, you drift back on any route that will take you there, and you encounter various writers—Jewish, Protestant, Catholic, Moslem, what have you. You begin to explore, and you bump into people like Aldous Huxley along the way and writers like Kazantzakis, with his lively sense of the miraculous. And great poets like Gerard Manley Hopkins, who is not only a remarkable Jesuit, but a remarkable man and a remarkable poet. If anyone ever celebrated creation as a poet, he certainly did. And people like Dylan Thomas who are rambunctious bums of the world, rambling through. And then you collide with people like George Bernard Shaw and his religious writings, his vast curiosity about the Life Force. All these amazing people impinge on your life; you begin to stir. Shakespeare comes in on you. And while he is not a philosopher in the usual sense—not an idea man in the sense of most idea men, like certain science fiction writers, or Aldous Huxley, or the French—he excites you with his sense of wonder.

Later you discover Melville, who takes Shakespeare the next mad step. And along the way Jules Verne! And Verne and Melville are two halves of the same coin. Suddenly you realize you've begun to think about the universe in terms of the way Melville does with his mad Captain Ahab. And his mad captain says he doesn't like the way God has put the cosmos together. He's going to strike through the mystery, smite the sun if it insults him, which is blasphemous. He is warned of this, and at the end of the book Ahab goes down with his ship for trying to solve the mystery with violence. Later, I get to thinking about Jules Verne and Nemo and his influence on my life when I was ten, twelve, thirteen. And Nemo is the reverse: he is the scientific method. He is the Christian who behaves to educate people to the ridiculousness of war. All people are holy. So he wants to take weapons away from people. In order to do this, he commits violence, but he's a big improvement on Ahab. For what Nemo says is instead of smiting the sun, plug into the sun, *use* the energy of the universe. Use the God-force to illuminate the deeps of the sea. So you can then harvest that sea. Nemo was Cousteau before Cousteau.

I'm the only essayist who has ever written a comparison between Nemo and Ahab. It's perfectly obvious. The evidence has lain there for a hundred years. At the start of *Twenty Thousand Leagues Under the Sea,* when the Nautilus appears for the first time, it is called The White Whale, Moby Dick. So we know then that Verne read Melville, and we know later in life that Melville read Shakespeare. How wonderful! This motion of ideas and glories from Shakespeare to Melville to Verne! With the latter two we share the two halves of experience, the two ways we feel about the universe as acted out by Ahab, who overreacts and strikes, or Nemo who plugs into the mystery and becomes a scientific searcher, moving to save people and harvest the sea; to love life rather than to detest the situation of mankind and the universe.

Thus, one day I found I'd grown into some sort of fourth-rate philosopher. I never started out that way. It evolved, and I discovered I was an original thinker by discovering the relationship between Nemo and Ahab which no one else had noticed.

But one captain is preferable to the other. Nemo celebrates life; Ahab destroys it. So I thought, hey, gosh, if I can have one original concept, I want to try for more. So I did the screenplay of *Moby Dick* over twenty-five years ago, and through it fell back in love with Shakespeare and the Bible. I get all these things that work on me. And I went and got a copy of the Old-New Testament while I was working on *Moby Dick* to find out who and how. I'd forgotten who Ahab was, who Ishmael was. I had to refresh my memory on all the biblical references and the Shakespearean ones, too. So I fell in love with language again, and I fell in love with concepts about the universe. It began to ferment in me.

Later on I discovered that Melville didn't read Shakespeare until he was thirty-one because he had poor eyesight. I've done a long poem on the impact of Shakespeare calling Melville's spirit forth like Lazarus from the tomb, saying, "Oh, Lazarus Herman Melville, truly come here forth and come here forth in a whale." So then Melville is birthed as the miraculous whale, called forth by Shakespeare. Terrific Shakespeare poetry. But Melville was working on a book about whaling, and Shakespeare happened to him and he threw the whaling book out the window and within a few short months Ahab and the White Whale were born! It's a biblical experience. It's titanic. So the effect of Shakespeare and Melville on each other, and then on me, was immense.

And then MGM came into my life when I was forty, and they were finishing the new version of *King of Kings*. And they said, "We want you to work on it, we have no ending for the film." I said, "You have no ending for the film? Have you tried the Bible?" And they said, "Well, yeah, but you know, there're four endings: Matthew, Mark, Luke, and John. Variations." So I said, "Okay, I'll come in for eight or nine weeks." They had no ending. They needed a history of the Jews up front to explain the concept of the Messiah so that when Christ comes on the scene you know what it's all about: why Caiaphas feels the way he does and why all those things happen to Christ—the jealousies, the power struggles, the whole thing of the Messiah who never arrives, at least, not for the Jews. So I did a history of the Jews for them up front, in the first five minutes, and I did the narration all the way through the film. I had a wonderful time with it because the Bible is filled with so much glorious language. I fell even more deeply in love with the Bible again. Of course, I've always been in love with the Book of Ruth and Job and Ecclesiastes because they taught me a lot about writing—the cadences, the beauty, the rhythm. I also did an ending for the film, an ending which they didn't shoot.

After that I wrote a play called *Leviathan* based on my experiences with *Moby Dick*, Shakespeare, the Bible, and along the way people like Kazantzakis. The whole story is *Moby Dick* in the future: the wonderful adventure of a mad captain of space, guided by a great white comet that came down through the universe when he was a young man and put out his eyes. Now very late in time he's going back out to confront the comet in deep space. His search leads him to discover that he and God are parts of the same thing.

As I found myself writing more and more about these things, I rediscovered a lot of Shaw. Shaw talks about the Life Force: what I like about it is that here on earth we are representatives of God, and that we are responsible for carrying the burden. I like to know that what I do is part of a large pattern, and therefore I must behave because I'm part of God. I'm not separate, and a lot of times various religions have, I think, made a mistake in separating us. Too often God has been put in a little matchbox on a shelf somewhere, or he's a label. He's off somewhere; he's not here. And when they do talk of him as here, they don't really prove it metaphorically. If they'd just say, look, God opens an eye and that eye is *you*—that's a good metaphor. I like being his eye. He is sensing himself, and I'm a part of another miracle.

When you go down to the sea and look at the multitudinous life forms, my God, it just continually drops your jaw, doesn't it? It's amazing. Have you ever seen a film on the birth of a kangaroo? Again, it's miraculous. Though its hind legs are not developed, the little kangaroo fetus crawls out of the womb, makes its way up the mother's belly, and blindly goes into her pouch and finishes its last fetal period attached to an udder in the pouch. The mother kangaroo doesn't birth it, doesn't help it, and if it falls off, that's the end. This miraculous little fetus crawling up her stomach and going into her pouch to finish its growth to me is so religious it's beyond speaking.

There are so many ways of teaching miracles through films that I think clergy and theologians are remiss in not finding them, particularly in wildlife films. There was a film that came out four years ago, the *Sexual Habits of Animals.* It sounds horrible on the face of it, and when you walk in and it starts you think, Oh my God, what am I going to see? Well, you see elephants copulating, hippopotami, rhinoceri, and swans, ducks, termites, ants, all kinds of spiders, but after a while it gets to be a glorious fecund explosion of the universe. You look, and you think, Wow! We have so many ways of surviving, so many shapes to take, so many ways of being. If I were a minister, a rabbi, or a priest, I would grab that film and take a chance and say to the people, "It's not what you think. Come on, take a look at these wonderful ways we have of filling the universe."

You know, Shaw was saying what Kazantzakis was saying: God cries out to be saved; we must save him. Now that has to be examined very carefully. It doesn't mean he really needs to be saved in quite the same way as it might sound. It's simply that we are one way of giving him eyes. He extends himself through the universe, and we represent his ability to see and feel and create in this part of the universe. That's beautiful. If we really believed that, we'd stop the wars tomorrow, wouldn't we? Stop offending one another, stop killing each other. But we don't believe it yet. I don't know what the answer is. I don't know how we can evolve toward that state where the various religions finally forgive each other and realize that we're all talking about the same thing, the same miracle, and we share it. We have these various tongues, and we fight over a metaphorical place, but it's really not all that important. The important thing is just being alive at all.

I wrote an essay for a book on philosophy that came out a few months ago. You know how we're continually surrounded by a lot of doomtalkers, end of the world people? To them I say, "Here's a test. Just imagine that you've been dead for a year, or fifty years, whatever. But in the middle of all this darkness we know nothing about what lies beyond. And God comes to you and says, 'Hey, how'd you like to be alive for one minute more, one minute more!' Which minute would you choose out of all the minutes of your life? And the answer is 'Any minute! Give me back a minute, I don't care which it is—a minute of pain, anything! Birth me again, give me a minute.'" It's that precious, that miraculous, and we forget. We forget to celebrate. We forget Scrooge thanking God it's Christmas morning and not beyond, and that he has a chance to save himself.

So, out of all these separate things comes a feeling that we are very special. A good part of the universe is empty. The molecules of the universe, the solar energy that comes out of the sun seems not to know itself. This table seems not to know itself. The molecules are all in there, they're not educated, and they cling together for very mysterious reasons. So much goes on in our bodies continually, yet we don't know the first thing about genetics—the mystery of how so many processes can go on within this skin every second and not run amok. It's beautiful. So, what I want to do by the end of my life is teach people to look better, to be responsible, and to do this without being a professional intellectual, without being stuffy, without boring others the way too many priests, rabbis, and ministers have done. If I could find the metaphors to do this, to give people back the gift of the miraculous, I would have had a good life. End of speech.

SWEENEY: That's not bad. It's exciting!

BRADBURY: You didn't expect that, did you?

SWEENEY: No, I didn't.

BRADBURY: Anything else you want to ask? Did we do all three questions? I don't know.

SWEENEY: I think you did. The third question: Who are you to God? you certainly alluded to when we talked about being the eyes of God or being the waking of God when he wakes; you were talking about that incredible union that we have with God, that, in a way, the activity of God on earth is through us now. And you also touched on the development of your consciousness of God as found especially in different metaphors and authors. You started in one section to describe briefly the place of Christ, or Jesus, in this—could you elaborate a little bit on that?

BRADBURY: Yeah, well, when people ask, was Jesus really the Son of God or was he a man, that really is like the old so-called fight between science and religion, which I believe is nonexistent. They're both doing the same thing: they're explaining the mystery. A scientist on a practical level still winds up utilizing faith. We try to explain gravity, but we don't know what it is; and we finally fall back on the faith of a theory which we hope will be constant. The sun burns but we don't know what light is. We have two or three theories of what light happens to be. So you end up with faith again; I don't care what you call it. You can call it theory, but it's still faith.

So we share an ignorance, don't we? Theologians and the scientists and all of us share an immense ignorance in the middle of all the glory. We should just close the territory. There's nothing to fight about; we all have to survive. Where the scientists leave off, the theologians take over, and vice versa. We can complement each other. I've watched the fight going on for years and thought "how stupid." No, we need each other: you can help me with my miracle, and I can help you.

But Christ to me . . . we are three billion Christs on this world and the sooner we realize that . . . . I wrote a poem which is in my *Book of Poetry.* The whole thing of mankind, of Christ being at the altar looking up and seeing mankind crucified, that's what it's all about, and until such time as we realize he was acting out something for us . . . Christ was saying, "What fools you are . . . really. What fools you are! You are crucifying yourselves by all your sins, everything that you do. You're driving the nails through your own hands, that's really what's happening." So the act of crucifixion here, to me, symbolizes mankind's torturing itself, killing itself. The whole act of war and destruction in the world is part of what Christ came here to teach us about, I think. But we have to stop it, really stop it, really believe that we are holy objects, every single one of us, holy not in any fake metaphorical sense but in a real sense. So in the poem Christ finally looks up and sees mankind pull out the nails, free himself from the cross, and go in peace. And with laughter he leaves them, accepting the universe. Then we can give up that part of the ritual.

We go into space and, of course, that's why I believe in space travel. Space travel is a religious endeavor and not a military one. It's not a technological feat. It's the attempt of mankind to relate himself to the universe. We have to go into space because we are the gift of this creation, and we can't stay here on earth. We're too important. So we have to move out through our solar system and go to other worlds, so that this particular portion of God will be spread throughout the universe, and our cognizance will be spread along with it. Maybe there's a super cognizance; we could say it's too big to encompass, it's too frightening, it's too total. So, all that we know now is that we are aware and alive, and we must protect that awareness. It's a very special gift, and we're surrounded by a lot of material that doesn't seem to be aware. Space travel, then, is a theological expedition whereby God in our shape goes through the universe. I've done a space age cantata on this with Jerry Goldsmith called "Christus Appollo" in which I say . . . let's see if I can find the poem for you. I'd like to read it:

Christ wanders in the Universe
A flesh of stars,
He takes on creature shapes
To suit the mildest elements,
He dresses Him in flesh beyond our ken.
There He walks, glides, flies, shambling of
      strangeness
Here He walks Men.

Among the ten trillion beams
A billion Bible scrolls are scored
In hieroglyphs among God's amplitudes of worlds;
In alphabet multitudinous
Tongues which are not quite tongues
Sigh, sibilate, wonder, cry:
As Christ comes manifest from a thunder-crimsoned
      sky.

He walks upon the molecules of seas
All boiling stews of beast
All maddened broth and brew and rising up of
      yeast.
There Christ by many names is known.
We call Him thus.
They call Him otherwise.
His name on any mouth would be a sweet surprise.

He comes with gifts for all,
Here: wine and bread.
There: nameless foods
At breakfasts where the morsels fall from stars
And Last Suppers are doled forth
With stuff of dreams.

So sit they there in times before the Man is
   crucified.

Here He has long been dead.
There He has not yet died.

SWEENEY: That's beautiful. Earlier, in the context of death, you
spoke about any moment of life being precious . . .
BRADBURY: Yeah, the whole thing, the total experience. It's
totally impossible, but here we are, and God is terrifying and
beautiful; and I wish people really believed that more. But I guess
a lot of people just want to be safe. They don't want . . . I'm not
criticizing them . . . each of us in his own way has to examine
what we have, and that's, of course, why you do have conflicts
between countries and religions. When you jar people's comfort,
when you make them think of the enormity of the universe and
how it goes on forever, that's terrifying, and they don't want to
think about that. They'd rather not study astronomy, even,
because it's frightening. They don't want to think of the miracle in
the way you and I are discussing it. That's where ritual helps them,
of course. They ritualize their lives in many ways; they get comfortable, which is fine, with their families. And there are rituals
with their families which are terrific and make us all feel good.

The burgeoning of life, of having your own children and watching them grow up duplicates of yourself. I have the sense of my
father being alive tonight in me, and that's a nice feeling to have on
occasion. It doesn't happen all the time, but once in a while when
the wind blows a certain way and I look at the hair on the back of
my hands, I sense his ghost in my flesh. And, of course, it is there,
and my mother, too. But, that's great. The sense of continuity, the
passing on of genetic information, that mysterious thing which is
the life ghost in each of us. I'd like to do more with all this in the
next fifteen or twenty years, if I have a chance.

GENE RODDENBERRY

The Star Trek series was one of the most popular ever produced for television. Woven throughout the marvelous stories of strange adventure and encounter with alien beings were profound sociological and psychological questions. I wondered what the producer of Star Trek, both the television series and the movies, would say about God. Gene invited me to his home for dinner with him and his wife, Majal. What a delightful evening it was—the company, the food, the conversation, Gene's inquisitive mind and lively imagination. It was a rare and charming occasion, the kind one holds in memory to bring a light of joy in more difficult times.

SWEENEY: What is God to you?

RODDENBERRY: I presume you want an introspective look at this. I think I've gone through quite an ordinary series of steps in life. I began as most children began, with God and Santa Claus and the tooth fairy and the Easter Bunny all being about the same thing. Then I went through the things that I think sensitive people go through, wrestling with the thoughts of Jesus—did he shit? Did he screw? I began to dare to believe that God wasn't some white beard. I began to look upon the miseries of the human race and to think God was not as simple as my mother said. As nearly as I can concentrate on the question today, I believe I am God; certainly you are; I think we intelligent beings on this planet are all a piece of God, are becoming God. In some sort of cyclical non-time thing we have to become God, so that we can end up creating ourselves, so that we can be in the first place.

11

I'm one of these people who insists on hard facts. I won't believe in a flying saucer until one lands out here or someone gives me photographs. But I'm almost as sure about this as if I did have facts, although the only test I have is my own consciousness.
SWEENEY: What's the primary plot that comes to your mind when you say that we are becoming God?
RODDENBERRY: I think God is as much a basic ingredient in the universe as neutrons and positrons; I suspect there is a scientific equation in matter and time and energy, and we'll ultimately discover the missing ingredient. God is, for lack of a better term, clout. This is the prime force, when we look around the universe.

I think God—we—(the equation of the universe) created time—our own beginnings and ends—so that we could exist. Let me explain what makes me think so: I think it's the very fact that I am the center of the universe, which is obviously so because everything in the universe comes to me via my sensations and impressions inside. And I hope it does to you, too. I hope you're not a trick someone is playing on me. I hope you have the same views. In that case, the universe is not really as simple as one universe, with one time sequence. It is a marvelously complex thing.

The very fact that through this thing I loosely describe as "thought" all this comes to me—my own experiences and also your experiences—this must mean that as certainly as two and two is four, God is the basic force behind creativity of life, and so on.
SWEENEY: Is it fair for me to summarize your thinking on God in this equation—God equals thought?
RODDENBERRY: God equals consciousness, yes.
SWEENEY: To take that one step further, can I conclude from this that in your life, when you have had an experience of God, it has been in terms of your increased consciousness, your increased exhilaration at being able to think?
RODDENBERRY: No. My experiences with the loose term "God" have not been a total sweep of understanding, but rather a slow putting together of a bit of this and a bit of that. God is a very personal and selfish concept to all of us, because we have no total

certainty. Yet putting together these small pieces is the beginning of the feeling of Godliness.

SWEENEY: There are some people who have divided human experience into mind, body, and spirit. When you say the word "thought," are you excluding from it feeling and emotion?

RODDENBERRY: I'm including it, completely. I think this Godliness that we're talking about is a part of pain, ecstasy, longing—all of these things which we only imperfectly realize and categorize.

SWEENEY: Can you point to one or two or three experiences in your life where you were able to say, "Ah, I think I have experienced God?"

RODDENBERRY: The first major experience of my life came rather late. I envy people who had it earlier. I went to a Baptist young people's Christian association, BYCU, which is about the ugliest title you could have for anything. They had by mistake invited a Scottish ex-minister who turned out to be, in the 1930s, a left-wing radical. He talked of new and exciting things, such as, wars were not just. And he said—this was World War I—the Germans were not Godless; God was not on our side. He really ridiculed the whole war. He introduced me to—I suppose not a very great book, but it was a revelation to me in those days— Pierre Van Paassen's *Days of Our Years*. And that was the first revelation in my life that things are not as they are said to be.

I met with him later. He took me to his apartment, in a hotel. My father was deathly afraid that I was being lured into a homosexual relationship, because what kind of man would invite a young boy to his apartment? He had a copy of the Koran there. To hear him say that this book was as holy as the one next to it, which is called the Bible, was a shocking and exciting thing. Yeah, that was a moment of taking a faltering step toward Godliness, I think.

SWEENEY: Is that *the* moment in your life, or are there others?

RODDENBERRY: Well, that was *the* one. It just caught me at the right time, the right moment of glandular secretions or whatever. I wanted to read everything on earth because this was such an exciting discovery. What there must be out there in all the libraries and bookstores!

I don't think I can remember any other experiences that were quite that huge. I suppose adolescent experiences must always have a hugeness about them.

SWEENEY: How old were you?

RODDENBERRY: Fourteen. I suppose the only experience similar to that came when I was creating the show *Star Trek* and thinking maybe I could do what Jonathan Swift did. When he wanted to comment on the English political system and do a satire on it, he had it happen to little people. Somewhere it occurred to me that I could make my comments, and if they happened to little purple people on far-out planets I could get it by my censors. And the idea began to grow in me that *Star Trek* adventures could be about many different "creatures" and events, so that I could get many different ideas by the censors on religion, on sex, on unions, on management, or on Vietnam, which was big on their minds at that time. There was in creating it—a moment of—shit, man, hey! I can do it! I can really think some things out and really say them.

SWEENEY: The experience that you relate is different from other things that I have read and other people I have talked to. They relate their experiences of God in terms of a person rather than in terms of an idea or an insight. How much of your experience of God has been related to a person as opposed to a heightening awareness, an idea, increased knowledge, and, of course, affection?

RODDENBERRY: I tend to ignore what I think you might want to hear.

My own feeling is that relating to God as a person is a petty, superstitious approach to the All, the Infinite. I remember as a young man being in Mexico City, at the Lady of Guadalupe Cathedral, I think it was. I watched the people crawl from ten miles away, from the city, with bleeding knees. I felt and understood that—at least to me—this was as foolish as the things I'd always laughed at on television when I saw the African tribesmen do the same thing. God is not a person, not a simple thing like that. I wish I could simply bleed or flagellate myself to get closer to him. But unfortunately it's not that easy. In fact, for many years I

was bitterly angry about people hurting themselves, and I cate-
gorized anyone who believed this way as stupid. I think that those
who find pleasure and relief in being at that—I was going to say
level, putting myself above them, but I don't mean that—if this is
the way they want to believe, and it gives them some understanding of themselves, then fine. God—whatever you are—bless
them, make them happy. For me it's not that simple. It's not an
individual. It's not even as simple as categories of good and evil,
because all we have to do is look in our backyard to find that all of
our systems of good and evil are denied by nature. It's a more
complex thing.

SWEENEY: Do you . . .

RODDENBERRY: I'm afraid of my answers. You ask me a simple
question and I go into a whole field.

SWEENEY: No, give me a direct answer. Don't worry about
whether it's contrary to my belief. But concerning what you
believe, do you communicate with God at all?

RODDENBERRY: I don't know. I see no reason to believe in, and I
don't believe in, psi factors, and cults, and things like that. But it
does seem that sometimes in the process of writing, in making
things happen, that sometimes you seem to get tuned in with
things. It's almost as if your receiver or transmitter were working
better. And ideas begin to come out of you that you're almost not
capable of. And certain things begin to happen that you somehow
know are right. Without for a moment equating myself with
Einstein, he said that in laying out relativity, certain things came
to him that he had to spend fifteen years working to prove, and
yet when they first came to him he knew they were right. Perhaps,
I think, the odds are slightly in favor that there is a mass consciousness, a transmitter somewhere that some of us occasionally
tune in to and get information that we have to spend many years
verifying.

SWEENEY: What difference does God make in your life?

RODDENBERRY: *I* would have to say, the concept of *being* God in
my life. . . . It's not anything to do with religion . . . it's the sense
that I belong . . . that I'm a part of it. And I cannot treat that
casually. I must try to become more a part of it and to understand
what my part of it means. It's much too important to just discard

by junking up, drinking whiskey, and smoking cigarettes—all of which I do. But in between there's the feeling that I am a part of something as important as the molecules that make all this up. And I ignore that at my own peril.

It's too marvelous, too. It's too marvelous to ignore and get tossed aside.

SWEENEY: Does your being God or your participating in God, whatever term you find appropriate, make a difference in such things as whether we drop bombs in Cambodia and drop bombs in Dresden? Does that make a difference?

RODDENBERRY: Oh, yes. It makes a great difference, and yet it doesn't make a difference. Let me try to explain that: I deny the bad logic, the stupidities that make . . . that create these things. I hate the fact that people who do it never thought of Godliness or obligation; or the fact that they are growing powerful and comfortable, while people who are more worthy of being part of this are dying and living in torture and pain.

At the same time, having worked in science fiction, which I think in some ways is a more interesting field than it has been given credit for, I've learned to take a longer perspective of all these things. I see a lot of this as the probably natural excitement and aggressiveness of an infant race growing up. If you're actually in Vietnam and flesh is burning up around you from napalm, it's got to be a horrible thing. But if you can take a few steps back from it—as indeed we do when we look at the story of the Roman Empire—I think you begin to see it as part of an infant God, an infant race, growing, lusty, shouting, slapping at each other in kindergarten. And I think that God or those nearer to God, another race, another intelligence slightly higher, look at us and say, "Well, the marvelously aggressive, healthy child is coming along." I think that races grow up the same way as children grow up. It can become something.

SWEENEY: How do you see us in the adult stage?

RODDENBERRY: That's—I was going to say that's the *one* thing, but I have to correct myself—that's one of *many* things that I haven't been able to resolve. In an adult stage will we achieve, or have thrust upon us, a oneness in which we are all cells in a great organism and a great mind, a great organism which is lofty and mature and wise and never does anything wrong? I'm afraid that might be rather dull. For me, at my level anyway, the sign of wisdom and maturity is being able to take delight in someone who says, "I disagree with you because." I think the worst possible thing that can happen to us is where all of us begin to act and talk and look and think alike. So I can see us moving toward that infinite oneness which is full of wisdom and peace and so on. And I find myself drawing back and saying, "Better we should have the loveliness of disagreeing." I don't want to play monopoly if my dice are perfect every time. I want to be able to say, "You're wrong. You prove to me you're right." At least I'll have the joy of proving that you're wrong. What loveliness!

It seems to me—it's likely that heaven's here right now. If you could take life with its pain and misery, where you fail and you sometimes win, and if you package it into a game, people would pay a fortune to have this game. And I don't know that I'd want it to be resolved so peacefully that the game would all be over.

SWEENEY: In several traditions of the world, people as Christians, or Hindus, or Buddhists, have a vehicle which they consciously direct to contact God—meditation or prayer or lifting up one's heart. Now, you did mention the act of writing, where sometimes you feel that some of the ideas are falling into your mind, coming from outside of you. This seems to be a bigger experience for you than any other to date. Is there any activity in your life that is a *conscious* attempt to be more of what you want to be, to get closer to this God ideal? Is there some vehicle that you use? Writing seems more of a passive thing. You were writing, then it was as though the muses were illuminating, or God was illuminating. . . .

RODDENBERRY: Writing takes you into a confrontation of self.

SWEENEY: Is there any other form, any other vehicle that you use?

RODDENBERRY: I tried Transcendental Meditation once and it didn't work particularly. It's very relaxing, but that's it. It was just a pleasant, floating lull. Like having pot. But you don't get busted for it! But as far as having lightning strike and saying, "Wow! I see it all!"—no.

No, there are no things I use. For the last fifteen or eighteen
years, my own way to get in touch, if indeed I do get in touch, has
been to train myself to wake up around five in the morning.
Strangely enough, you can do it without an alarm clock. I read for
two—two and a half hours—before the family wakes up. The
books I've read recently range from trashy literature to a new
Oxford study of the life of Alexander the Great; *No Time to Die;
Attica; Helter Skelter; The Study of Cromwell*—and just whatever
reading happens to come along. I always read *Playboy* cover to
cover and wish I were younger and could try some of those
things. I read every morning, and it just sort of gets my engine
going, so that by the time I get outside, and walk around, and take
a swim when the weather's right, and get to my desk, everything is
going and I write better. The only other thing I use is going out
lecturing at colleges. Kids ask me embarrassing questions and
you really have to—I'm sure the same thing happens to you—you
have to ask, "Did I give the right answer?" I never really re-
examined my whole thinking because wow, that was tough. And
that's good for a writer.

SWEENEY: What do you think of one of the documents in history
which is the New Testament?

RODDENBERRY: I think there is almost clearly a divinity, a concept which is in these things. But I think that this is probably true
of almost all serious writing. I think that the Bible is probably no
more divine than Shakespeare or *Naked City* or anything. You
have to search for divinity. You have to find it and analyze it. I can't
conceive of whatever God is, going down and pointing the finger
and saying, "Okay, for this particular publisher you've got
divinity." I think that you see it in *Walden Pond* and *Leaves of
Grass* and no doubt in Oriental and Indian and other things that
we're not even familiar with.

SWEENEY: What about the Bible's explicit claims of Christ's
divinity?

RODDENBERRY: Well, my feeling about Jesus, which has gone
from the things I talked about in boyhood in a church which
probably held Jesus as more divine than the Catholic Church
holds him—you know, "Sweet Jesus," "Jesus wants me for a
sunbeam"—it has gone from that to almost an affirmation for me

that I am God. It seems to me that everything he said is, "I am, and you are." He did a better job of it than I've done. But, you know, many people do better things than I do. Yes, I think he was in closer contact. I think, to me the whole joy and glory of Jesus is the fact that he is one of us. It seems to me that the whole statement of the New Testament is, "Hey, man, you can too, because I was born like you. I died like you. There's nothing special about me that's not special in you. And I'm offering you both." And I think this divinity thing is bullshit because they've taken away from the glorious, divine message that he kept saying over and over again. Divine, yes, but so are we. I think that's what he was saying: "So are you."

SWEENEY: There's a book by Alan Watts called *Beyond the Spirit.* Have you read it?

RODDENBERRY: No.

SWEENEY: If you ever have the chance. . . .

RODDENBERRY: I don't read religious things very much because I got burned by them so badly as a child. I think this is true of many people. I know it doesn't make sense, but it is getting burned. And you sort of turn your back on it, and if they can sneak you religious stuff without your really knowing that it is, like I read a beautifully religious book on my last trip called *The Kapillan of Malta* or something like that. A story of a priest—oh, yes, it's a beautiful book. I'll loan it to you before you leave if you like. The story of a simple priest who turned out to be not so simple because of his inner strength. It took place in the days of the blitz and all that, and showed how he led his people, these villagers that lived in the catacombs. The hierarchy of the church hated him because there was the shit and smell of fish soup and the people lived on the ledges where they had taken the saints' bodies away so that these people could live, sleep, and make love. And he was saying, "This is life. This is how it is. I cannot change my people. All I can do for them is love them, bind them when they bleed." And finally as he was dying people began to realize, "Hey, wait a minute. This is more Christ-like than any of the high bishops that look down their noses at him." It's a lovely book.

SWEENEY: This lobster dinner was terrific. So was the interview. I'm really grateful.

RODDENBERRY: Me, too. It's been fun.

MARTIN SHEEN

__Missiles of October__, __The Catholics__, __The Execution of Private Slovak__, __Apocalypse Now__, the Kennedy miniseries, and the television production __Blind Ambition__—these are just a few of the many shows in which Martin Sheen has acted. Martin is friendly, genuine, and vibrant.

SWEENEY: Who is God to you?

SHEEN: I was raised in a Catholic family. My father was Spanish, my mother Irish. And our image of God, the angels, the saints, and what have you, you know, was a very spiritual one. What they looked like was never really clear to us. We made our contact with God, so to speak, through Christ. You know, we received Christ in communion, we were told that this was the most important thing in our lives.

But when I was very young, I saw that other people weren't stirred in the same way my family was. One Good Friday in our parish church, they had a procession for a relic of the true cross. And everybody got terribly excited about this, this splinter from the true cross. It was deposited on a side altar and venerated. And I remember I was a little confused because here we were told how important this relic was, a splinter of the true cross. But at the same time, we were permitted, in Holy Communion, to receive the very one who died on that cross. And there didn't seem to be as much excitement about receiving communion as there was about the relic. And I think that had a lesson. For me, at any rate. I saw it was easier for people to believe in something they could touch or see, relate to in human terms. It's so much more difficult to do it spiritually.

Later, I expanded my image of God's spirit still further. I was
able to do this without qualms because during my teen years—
when most people question religion anyway; there's no one
insisting that they go to Mass, to confession, and they don't feel so
afraid to examine, to question—the Ecumenical Council was just
being convened; and Pope John was in the (I wanted to say the
White House) was in the Vatican. He was the symbol of great
change. In the Baltimore Catechism, we had been taught never to
question, to accept it on faith. But now people were questioning,
and dogma wasn't so pat.

The image I grew to have of God's spirit is that God can be
perceived in the actions and feelings of human beings. When the
Vietnam war was near its peak and children were being bombed
and killed—innocent people are always being mutilated—I
talked to a spiritual person. (When I say spiritual I mean someone
on another spiritual level, higher than what is considered normal;
not religious but aware.) And this person told me that when you
feel the loss of a stranger's child as if it were your own, then you
have been in touch with God. And that is a tremendous thing. But
I see that we all have something in ourselves that feels this way.
How did you feel when you first saw the pictures—not only the
still photographs, but newsreel footage of the children running
naked from the villages, mothers carrying naked babies, skin
burned, weeping, and refugees caught in a terrible fight, burned
and mutilated and running, crying? I know everybody was terribly moved and hurt. So this proves to me that none of us are so far
from God. All of us are very close.

Here's a tragic story: Less than two months ago a friend of mine
was helping me dig a trampoline pit in the backyard for the kids.
He's been a Christian. He's accepted Christ from the Bible, not
attached to a religion *per se.* And he's always trying to hook me,
you know, to get into Bible study class. Very sincere. And as we
were digging, he said, "You know, my son went to Vietnam. He's
nineteen years old." I said, "Gee, why did he go?" "Because he
volunteered. He believed that they were godless people and they
should be punished." Now just stop and think about that and
think of how many went there for that reason. Those "Communists." Those "ungodly" people. God gave us the right to kill them.

We're in charge. Now that's taking a personal, limited image of God and using it to destroy another person's right to live. Or to force yourself to be inhumane to another human being. Now, I've often thought—the thought has been expressed before—but if we all had to fight naked, we wouldn't be able to identify them. Or with paper bags over our heads. We'd have to regroup and end up with some people on each side. The image of God that my friend is using is the one of the ancient Bible, where God gave the Israelites lots of power over other people. You are talking about a merciful God, but still, he slammed down this group over here, and favored this group over there. It doesn't really follow Christ's teachings: "I came here not to wear any crowns. I'm not going to lead you to any kingdom. My kingdom is not of this world. It's on a spiritual level." They didn't know what he was talking about. They were looking for someone to come and smash. A prejudiced God. We've seen that same sort of thing right in our own backyard. Reverend King said, "I feel sorry for you because you don't like me just because I'm black. Because if you saw my spirit, you know, you would identify with it."

If you were from Afghanistan or Vietnam or some other culture, although we couldn't understand certain things about each other, we could still relate on a spiritual level—on how we dealt with other people. I would see you among your friends and say, "Here's a fine man. A lovely man." You'd say, "Well, I try to be kind and courteous and friendly." So all of us have got the connecting spirit, I think. But we distract ourselves. We're greedy about our lives. We're even greedy about God. We all try to possess him by seeing him in physical terms, in non-spiritual terms. It's so much easier. We give him a gender. We give him a place. We insist he be limited to the way *we* want him to be.

If we would just accept that we are in touch with God, we couldn't help but use that as a reason to make direct contact with other human beings. Then we'd have a new attitude towards people, where if we'd see someone doing something we call bad, instead of condemning—which is what we're taught—we'd have empathy. We'd condemn or punish not that person, but what he did, and really feel sorry for that person. We'd say, "They're in trouble because they're out of touch with themselves."

Actors have a great opportunity to be religious in this way: in a sense they always live close to their own feelings; part of those feelings is the spiritual feeling, the imagination. If we can't imagine, if we can't make believe, we can't act.

For years, as an actor, it never occurred to me that I was living my life in a spiritual sense. but I have a friend, a fellow actor, who is very spiritual—Gene Roche. He is very devout, very concerned, always interested in new ideas and exploring. And once we were talking, and he said, "You know, acting is a very spiritual profession. Have you ever thought of that?" I hadn't thought of that. To me it was just a means of making a living doing something I enjoyed very much. But Gene whetted my appetite for this kind of thinking. I began to dwell on this, to relate to it. And I realized, it's true. We really do expand the spirit in a way that goes beyond entertaining. Once Gene said, "What do you think would happen if all the actors and all the artists disappeared from the world?" And I hadn't thought of it. He said, "I think the world would die; because it would be the end of the spirit." He's right. Our imaginations would not be encouraged to grow, to go beyond horizons that we know exist. They would wither. The spirit and the imagination seek new horizons; they are part of the same thing.

SWEENEY: Do you pray at all?

SHEEN: Only when I get in trouble. I'm hypocritical in that regard. If I'm on the freeway, for example, and I'm late, I say, "Oh, dear God, let that car pass me so I can sneak and get under. . . ." You know. I'm always doing that.

SWEENEY: But where do you direct that prayer, if the image that you see in your mind is divinely human?

SHEEN: Where is that prayer directed? It just . . . goes. I feel like I'm making contact. I don't feel that I'm talking to myself when I pray. I don't think people who pray do, do they? If they're really praying, they are in touch with an Other, which I think is God, or part of God, or at least the presence of God in us.

I think we would be a bunch of morons if we didn't really believe that we were making contact somewhere with some higher form, some spirit, some . . . I want to say "one," but there is not "one" per se. It's higher than that.

SWEENEY: You mentioned a couple of really profound insights that were given to you by a fellow actor and also a rather significant insight you had as a young child. Have you had any other experience either while praying or in your contacts with other people when you felt clearly that God had touched you?

SHEEN: It's difficult to put a direct line to one incident. It's only afterwards that I look back and think, well, maybe when I loved my child or my wife, or when I was helpful to my neighbor. But you do it because it's the right thing; a lot of good in the world is done because you don't want to incriminate yourself. You help the fellow on the side of the road because you're reminded that if something bad happens to him, I'm going to be responsible. So it's not really pity or compassion or empathy; it's really kind of a selfish thing we do, in a sense, to avoid that happening. But that too is a communion on the spiritual level. You are doing a Christian thing.

SWEENEY: Let's get back to your seeing the death of another person's child as your own. *The Brothers Karamazov,* by Dostoyevsky, talks about Aloysha's mystical vision, that his actions and love had reverberations throughout the world.

SHEEN: Sure, I can understand that. Unfortunately, I didn't read that. For many years I've been told to read that book, but I never have. I didn't know it was such a spiritual book. You know, that's a very interesting statement. It's close to a theory of mine that is not particularly popular, but it goes along with a lot of what's happening in spiritualism and mediumship and so forth, the theory that we reincarnate, that we reach higher and higher levels until we understand that all people are connected into one spiritual family. I know the church doesn't say the reincarnation idea is kosher, because we are responsible for our own actions. But the basic theory might really *be* in line with the church—life everlasting, resurrection of the dead. When you think of it in terms of each human being on the face of the earth having had a spirit that existed from all time. . . . You can even trace that back to the Bible, when God created the different angels. Isn't that part of the Testament?

SWEENEY: Well, in the Old Testament they don't go into the creation of angels. That comes from Milton and several other classics in English literature. Creation in the Book of Genesis only talks about the creation of the world, matter, and man and woman. There are several instances in the Old Testament where there are angelic figures appearing. But as to when or how angels were created. . . .

SHEEN: There is a lot of discussion about a group that was given some sort of a choice. And Lucifer took one side, and Michael took the other side, right?

SWEENEY: That comes out of Milton's *Paradise Lost,* and the Book of Revelation.

SHEEN: Oh, I thought it was from the Old Testament. At any rate, I connect the existence of angels with the theory that we all lived before, and the only way we can get back on the godly plane, the highest plane, is to purify ourselves. I'm not saying I believe this, but I consider this possibility. We have all lived before, all of us. And we're back each time, you know, to purify ourselves. We make the same mistakes, and we take the human form again, and we make the same mistakes.

Now it's curious what's happening in this latter part of the twentieth century. Because it is said that a soul will reincarnate every twenty years. Now before the Vietnam situation there was World War II, and a lot of souls were wrenched from the globe during World War II. And it is a theory that they came back, so furious that their lives had been taken away from them so young and so much against their will, that they all came back and that's why we had such a huge protest against Vietnam. This is something we *can* relate to.

And the theory isn't so far off from Catholicism. They never refer to death as being the end, but the continuation of the spirit. The whole point of Christianity is that the spirit exists; it was created by God, given us to go through this life. In our lifetime we do see certain people we somehow feel are on their last journey. Not all of them are public figures but some of them have been, I think. Reverend King was. Maybe Father Damien among the lepers. Maybe Mahatma Gandhi. Maybe the Rosenbergs. Maybe, you know, Dreyfus; maybe Slovak. Maybe these people were ready. They were purified. They were beyond physical things.

They had reached the level where they were ready to experience being with God, to purify their spirits there.

SWEENEY: Traditional Catholic theology says there was a time when man did not exist. He is born, he lives his life, and only after death does he enter eternity. But in several Eastern religions they believe in several levels of reincarnation; sometimes a person comes back in the form of a lower species, sometimes as a human. And there are levels of purification, as you say. It would be very interesting to compare that kind of reincarnation theology with Christian teachings on afterlife, purgatory, the resurrected body. In the past, religions have made a big deal of their theological differences; but really when you get down to it, tracing the common elements, there's so much in common.

SHEEN: Striving towards communicating spiritually, in any religion, seems to me to have at its essence driving toward one thing, peace. Peace and tranquility. "Peace be with you" is the last thing the priest says to you as you exit the confessional. How many of us are really at peace? How often in our lives are we really at peace? Not concerned, not worried, really at peace? I think it's something that all religions, all beliefs, all faiths have absolutely at their core. When you see the looks on evangelists' faces— whether it's acted or not—their followers are convinced that that person is at peace. I think that's what they desire most of all. I think all human beings do. We live in such turmoil in our day-to-day lives. I don't mean only in wartorn countries—in physical struggle—but in our everyday lives we struggle to obtain peace. It's extraordinary. I think how many times during the day am I really, really at peace? It's a rare thing.

But I guess to get peace you have to forget the physical— comforts, things. Look at some of the church's champions, like Francis of Assisi and his followers. I mean, look how far they went. Even the church of the time said they had gone to the point of absurdity. But were they not doing what Christ had asked? Father Berrigan, who was arrested after Catonsville, was told by one of his followers, "Father, you go to jail. You don't have a family. Do you expect all of us with families to go to jail?" Berrigan said, "Yes." The other said, "What would happen to our children if we went to jail?" Berrigan had reached the level of commitment, not attached to anything but his follower was wavering.

When you begin to think how many things we're attached to, it's absurd—the car and other material things. I'm not talking about personal or emotional attachments, just things. I think basically they're distractions. They get in the way. They clutter up; we carry so much luggage. If someone told you right now you were going to die, you wouldn't even think about your money or possessions. You'd think about your loved ones. Of course, you'd want to pass on something. I guess I'd think of saying, "Make sure they get the money," but I tend to think my very last thought would be on trying to create peace, trying to square an account somewhere. It wouldn't be a material account. It's fascinating.

Francis is one of my favorite figures. But he couldn't work within the structure of the church. It's an actual fact. He was too spiritual. He didn't want to own property. He didn't even want to own the clothes on his back. He didn't even want to die on a bed; he wanted to die on the floor. He was totally free, totally unattached to material things. I think this was the essence of God in him.

Christ's whole bag was peace. When I see these wild zealots preaching, they're in a turmoil. Maybe sincere, but crazy. What's coming off? It's tension. It's like my friend—it's tragic—to use God to such an extreme; to pass it on to your children; to say this is your duty. If people would only see God spiritually, not physically, maybe we could reach that peace.

DOROTHY DAY

Social activist, journalist, publisher, Dorothy Day helped found St. Joseph's House of Hospitality in New York City, and many other houses and farms for the poor and homeless. She was co-founder of the Catholic Worker Movement, and is thought by many to be the most influential person in American Catholicism. This telephone interview was brief as her doctor had ordered her to rest. She died on November 29, 1980.

DAY: . . . I say that because I've just been reading a book on Russian writers, and they said what brought them to a sense of faith was the Creation itself. A lot of the young Russian poets are writing religious verse and the very word Creation, of course, made me feel a great sense of awe in God's creation. We are living in a very beautiful place up here on the Hudson River. We have a constantly majestic river passing right by our windows. It's so beautiful, and the hills across the river—you can't help but feel, you know, this sense of God's creation and the fact that you are part of it.

SWEENEY: Have there been any major changes in your experience of God?

DAY: No, I think I have a pretty even existence. Trying to get to daily Mass, or spending a certain amount of time every day in prayer. Saying the Rosary and the Jesus prayer.

SWEENEY: What I'm getting at is this: in your lifetime have there been two or three major shifts in your attitude on God, or has it been pretty steady all the time?

DAY: Pretty steady. I think I started very young, as a matter of fact, when I was a child. Coming across the Bible. I used to go around to different churches on Sunday morning and I wanted to be a

Catholic. But my father said go to my mother's church, which was Episcopalian. They gave me a great deal. They gave me the Psalms, the Canticles, and I used to go regularly from then on. Oh, then, of course, in my college years I think I considered myself an agnostic. I think that is, you know, something that every young person goes through.

SWEENEY: How do you see God?

DAY: As a personal God. Question the Scriptures, the life of Jesus. I think the present Pentecostal movement has done a tremendous amount to revive that sense of healing power, the practice of the presence of God.

SWEENEY: And, a question that might be a little more difficult to answer: Who do you think you are to God?

DAY: As children. I've got nine grandchildren and twelve great-grandchildren, and I know how I feel about all of them. I mean, every new baby that comes into the family is *so precious*. A baby was born on the fourth of July to my daughter, living here on the farm with us. She has three. So I'm in close contact with my family. I feel that the family is the unit of society, and I think we've all stuck together pretty well.

SWEENEY: So you think you are to God a child?

DAY: Yes, very much so. I think we're constantly being taught. I think we're learning every day.

SWEENEY: Well, thank you very much. I hope that you get well, that you recover from this latest heart attack.

DAY: Well, this is sort of a blessing, I'd say, because I have time to read, to study, to do more writing, and it's, well, it's a great joy.

SWEENEY: Is there any one statement that you would consider very important to tell people about God?

DAY: I think to read the words of Jesus in the New Testament. We should constantly be turning to the Sermon on the Mount and testing it. The Lord's Prayer. Pope John said the Lord's Prayer had everything in it.

I like to read his letters to the family. A good practical man in many ways. All these things came out, the tremendous simplicity of his faith.

SWEENEY: Yes, Pope John was an extraordinary man.

DAY: He certainly was. A peasant, close to the land. Somebody swiped my diary, you know the paperback copy of Pope John's *Journal of a Soul.* I've got his letters to his family, but I haven't got his Journal. Now could you go ahead and see if you can find me his Journal?

SWEENEY: Okay. Where do you want me to send it?

DAY: To Tivoli, New York. . . . See, I'm always a beggar. You know the saying, "Love is an exchange of gifts"?

SWEENEY: Yes, I do.

DAY: So, you can—when I'm being a beggar like this—you can just say we've had this little interview on the phone and so I want you to send me this gift.

SWEENEY: That's exactly what I'll do.

DAY: Good.

SWEENEY: Thank you very much.

DAY: All right, thank you. Bye.

FRANK CAPRA

Frank Capra has produced and directed many films including Arsenic and Old Lace, Mr. Smith Goes to Washington, It's a Wonderful Life, Lost Horizon, It Happened One Night, Pocketful of Miracles, *and* Mr. Deeds Goes to Town. *Three times he received Academy Awards for best direction of the year, and two of the pictures he produced won Oscars.*

SWEENEY: How has your relationship with God changed over the years?

CAPRA: Have you read my book, *The Name Above the Title*?

SWEENEY: I've read about a hundred pages, and I'm reading the rest of it.

CAPRA: Well, when I was a kid, my family was very religious, and they would drag me off to church, and I got funny impressions of it. We belonged to a very poor parish; we confessed our sins; I used to sell papers downtown to very rich people. But I didn't see these people in church; I didn't see them confessing their sins. So, in my mind I equated the Catholic Church as the religion of the poor, because only poor people went, and only the poor seemed to commit sins. And somehow I thought, aha! our sin is that we're poor. The rich didn't have to go to confession; they didn't have to do anything. These were the kinds of things that just cooled me off as far as the church was concerned.

Another thing: My father had a shoe shine stand. I sold papers, and sometimes we'd walk home together. And every time we passed the Plaza Church, he took off his hat. And I had to take off whatever cap I had. And I said, "What do we do this for?" And he says, "Well, we show respect to God." And I . . . for God's sakes, I mean, I looked and nobody else was doing it! And so that grew on me. I had to take off my hat every time I went by there on a streetcar or a bicycle or whatever. And I used to go 'round the block not to do it, 'cause I felt very silly; I felt it was not right that I should take off my hat to a building. My early experiences of the Catholic Church were not very appetizing, as far as I was concerned. That was because I didn't know enough about it, but I am a very religious man secretly.

So I tried other churches, like Christian Science; and I tried all kinds of religions throughout my life. But none of them could hold me. The Protestant churches didn't appeal to me at all. The biggest thing was the money collection.

Christian Science appealed to me for quite a while, though, because it was a Christian Scientist who woke me up to the whole thing about religion. After I shook the Oscar tree with *Mr. Smith Goes to Washington,* I was afraid to make another film because where could I go? I'd already made it. I'd climbed Mount Everest. I could only go downhill. And yet I had a contract to make two films a year that I had to fulfill. And they had already sold these pictures before they were made. So there was this pressure to keep making films, and I didn't think I could make anything to top that film. Where would I go after this thing got all the Oscars? I just wanted to quit.

So I decided to get sick. I talked myself into becoming sick. And I was practically dying, when a friend of mine brought this stranger to me who said, "You're an offense to God and to man. God gave you these gifts, these talents you have. You have no right to use them or not use them at your own liberty. You've been given them to use, and when you don't, you're an offense to God and to man." That's what he said. And of course, he was exactly right. My sickness was a big act.

So that started me thinking, and of course, God became very real. As soon as I began to believe and understand that whatever gifts I'd been given were not mine, that made some sense to me. I could understand Mozart, I could understand Beethoven, I could understand lots of people who had these wonderful gifts, and certainly they didn't come out of their genes—their parents didn't have any of these gifts and things. Where did this creativity come from that people have? Where does mine come from? Why this spirit? Why these hunches? Where do hunches come from? They don't come from mathematics, they don't come from reading, they don't come from study of any kind.

SWEENEY: When this man walked in and said, "You're an offense to God" how old were you?

CAPRA: I was almost forty years old. It turned me completely around, everything I did from that time on I realized was my way of saying, "Thank God!" Or, "Thank America" for having brought my family here.

SWEENEY: So, your talent, your using your talents, was your way of saying, "Thank God."

CAPRA: Right.

SWEENEY: And did this draw you closer to the Catholic Church, or did this draw you closer to God?

CAPRA: It drew me closer to God, of course, but it also drew me closer to the Catholic Church. Because of all the things that I try, nothing seems to give me the feeling that the Mass does. There are times you go to Mass and you feel, "Yeah, I was there, I put in the time," and it really hasn't made much of a difference. But once in a while you go to Mass, and you kneel, and suddenly the whole damn thing opens up and you lose sight of everything else around you, and you get a glimpse of that eternal. And maybe only for a moment, maybe only for ten seconds, but you do see that eternal. It may happen to you once every hundred Masses. And when it happens it leaves you shaking, cleansed in some way, and—to know there's something to this thing, you know it's there—you can't explain it, can't express it, but you can feel it.

SWEENEY: Is there anything comparable to that experience of the eternal that you found while making films?

CAPRA: Oh yes. What is making films? Making films is a judgment of values. Why is this scene better than the scene before? And so on. Value decisions, judgment decisions, creative decisions— these you make just out of pure guts, they come from nowhere. And so, it's the same kind of thing. You're dealing in the intangibles. But it's not so intangible when it gets done; it's a very concrete thing when it comes out.

SWEENEY: There is a distinction between intuitive knowing and rational knowing; an intuitive knowing is a direct or immediate apprehension of a good or the true, just chboom! like that, without any logical process. Is that what you mean by gut decision?

CAPRA: That's right. It's a hunch. Hunches have no rationalization whatever. And in creativity, you must follow the hunch. Not the form sheet. Because that hunch is trying to tell you something, and you've got to follow it. Now, it may lead you down some strange track, but you've got to follow it because you've got to believe in it more than you do the form sheet.

All creative people live by hunches. Live by creativity. Creativity comes from the word creator in the first place, and, you know, in a sense you're doing God's work, or you're acting as a little god on earth when you're creating something that did not exist before. Whether you're writing a book, or painting a painting, or whether you're building a building, or teaching—you're creating.

SWEENEY: Who is God to you?

CAPRA: Well, I can't tell you. When I was a child God was a man with a beard. I imagined him as a very venerable old guy who knew everything, had been through everything, and who had been the wise man of all time. As I got into the creative business, then I realized that creativity and God were connected, directly connected. Whether you believed in God or not. You had to believe, if you believed in creativity, you had to believe in some creator. And if you believed in some creator, where do you end up? You must go to that prime creator, Number One Man, Number One Idea, Number One Happening, whatever it is. There's a prime mover to this thing, a prime creator, which has set our universe in motion. Things are too ordered in the universe to be the results of chaos. The fact, for instance, that everything in the universe is in motion, nothing ever stands still. There is thought to this thing somewhere, there is order, and there is guidance. Now who can that be?

However you take man—whether he came from the apes, or whether he was singled out by God from the dust and mud— however it happens, there is no way you can get away from the fact that there's got to be some sort of divine idea to the whole thing.

SWEENEY: How does that divine idea relate to you?

CAPRA: I think, I am a sensitive person, I am a perceptive person, I feel, I have ideas, I remember, I can create. I create things that haven't existed before. I can be compassionate. In a sense, there is divinity in all life, in all matter; and so I'm certainly a piece of God, a very small, ugly piece of God, but I'm a piece of God. I know when I'm compassionate, and I know when I'm a mean stinker. So that I place value judgments on my own behavior. I know good from evil, and I know right from wrong. Now, who gives me that? Where did I get this feeling of right from wrong? So there must be some divinity within me.

SWEENEY: Have there been moments in your life when you have felt that either through your talent, or through your ideas, or through your feelings, you have been in contact with God? You mentioned you have felt moments where eternity opened up. Are there moments when you have felt something more personal, in the sense of not simply a profound feeling of something that was infinite and incomprehensible, but an experience topped with the knowledge that this is of God, and this is God?

CAPRA: Well, I think . . . that perhaps when I go into a theater and I see one of my films playing, and there are a thousand people in that theater, and they're all intensely interested in what is going on, completely involved, and they're either being entertained or being moved, or being exalted, then such a wonderful feeling comes over you of accomplishment, or achievement, that you're able to do this. And when you see these people go out of the theater feeling better, perhaps *being* better persons for having seen that thing, then you must in a sense become mystic at that time. You have a very powerful weapon in your hand, a very powerful tool for entertaining, enlightening, exalting, inspiring people. And there it is, you see it happening. You see the physical, the expression of that idea right in the theater. You see it happen. Well, I don't know that I can see God in that, but I can see God in that process, somewhere. And I can see that we've taken one step further away from the jungle because of that particular event there and feel we're evolving toward the spiritual because of it.

SWEENEY: Have you ever had an experience where you understood what you meant to God? Or how God looked upon you?

CAPRA: Pardon? Say that again?

SWEENEY: Have you ever had an experience where you understood how God looked upon you, what you meant to God? And if I can phrase it another way, how important do you feel you are to God? How do you think God looks upon you? If God were describing Frank Capra, how do you think he would do it?

CAPRA: Well, I think once in a while he'd smile, because I've made so many other people smile, you know, in the films, comedy, especially. I think he'd enjoy that. And, perhaps I think he'd have a feeling that I've been doing his work in a way. Because films are a people to people communication. They are actors or human beings communicating to other human beings; and perhaps at times, he says, "By golly, this film is a hell of a thing. This guy is doing some good with his film, maybe more good than a lot of priests are in church." I feel that, of course. I feel that strongly. That's why I am so, let's say, humble about these things, this talent that was given me, and how I'm pretty sure it was given me by some divinity. And therefore I should use it. But there are many ways for God to express himself to people, through people, and I'm sure that when a child is born, there is a new thing born. When a new plant comes up, when a little puppy is born, there is an ongoing thing—something divine, something we can't understand, yet there's something that we adore and admire, and are inspired by. The presence of something divine is there.

SWEENEY: One of the things that comes out very clearly in Christian tradition is that people who are profoundly Christian somewhere along the line end up having to carry their cross: "If you're going to follow me, take up your cross." Is there one experience, or one realization more than any other that you would characterize as your cross?

CAPRA: Well, my cross is not being able to retire from this—not to be able to say to this talent, "Go away, I'm finished with you. I want to enjoy myself now. I want to play golf, I want to do this, I want to do that." No, you can't do that. And your cross is the talent you have. It is with you constantly. It bugs you, and it keeps you going, keeps you thinking, keeps you from becoming satisfied with yourself. You're never satisfied, never. There are always things you should be doing and ought to be doing. And it gives you this drive. You can't let go of it. You can't turn it off. No way to turn it off, there's no way to say, "I'm through. Finished. Goodbye. I'm going to Hawaii, get on an island, and the hell with it." So I suppose the cross that creative people bear is the ability to create. And, when they don't create—it's their cross. Their cross is not being able to drop it!

SWEENEY: How would you describe yourself?

CAPRA: Well, I guess I would describe myself more as a pioneer, always wondering what it's all about. I'm happy, because I've been given the opportunity to express myself, and to pass my wondering on to other people. I feel part of the universal creativity, and in a sense that gives me a great sense of belonging, of being with it, being with it no matter what happens, because it makes me— rather than a cynic—a lover of people.

EDGAR MAGNIN

President of the Wilshire Boulevard Temple in Los Angeles and one of the leading spokesmen for Jewish communities in the western states, Rabbi Magnin is a delightful blend of charm, good humor, faith, strong convictions, and humility.

SWEENEY: Well, you began qualifying the questions right away by indicating that intelligence can reach only so far in terms of faith. And because faith in God really involves a reality that is beyond human expression and knowledge, any terms or expressions that are used fall short of the God reality.

MAGNIN: Yes. There are some things you never can explain or state. Poets sometimes do, in their way. For instance, take the love of a mother or father for a child: If any parent had to sit down and analyze his love for his child, he couldn't do it. You know by what he does, by how he feels, but he can never put that into words. So it's impossible to put into words just what our concept of God is, because we have a limited intelligence. Man's mind is above the animals but stops at a certain point. And then we're up against a stone wall because God—if there is God, and I believe there is—is infinite and eternal and beyond human finite dimensions. And it was Maimonides in the twelfth century, the famous Jewish philosopher, physician, and rabbi, who said that whatever appellations we use about God are purely limited. We say God is good. That means what *we* think is good.

God is something I feel. I know him, not in the sense that I know this is a piece of paper, or this is my watch on my wrist, but I know him because I feel that he is there. In other words,

I'm one of those creatures who believes in intuition. Our knowledge comes partly though the five senses: taste, feeling (feeling is touch), smell, sight, hearing. But God is something that goes beyond those five senses. You can't hear God's voice in the sense in which you hear a human voice. We don't see God in the way in which you look at a person or a building or something of that sort. And yet I have very deep religious convictions; I *feel* this thing intuitively; I *know* this exists, that which we call God, and I have no desire to try to invent all kinds of reasons for my faith or try to use appellations that really are not accurate.

I was listening to an interview with Arthur Rubenstein, and somebody asked, "Do you believe in God?" (I'm trusting memory now.) I believe his answer was something like mine: "I know there is a God, but I can't explain it." They asked him if there is a soul. He said, "Well, I don't know whether there's a soul or not, but one time I was playing Chopin, and something was touching my fingers, moving my fingers." This little bit of mysticism is something I think every artist feels. And that's the way I feel.

For instance, when I speak I prepare, I have notes; I may have an outline, but most of the time I don't look at them. I'm exactly like a piece of wire through which electricity moves. This sounds strange, but it's true. When I'm most effective, I become . . . used by something. Now this sounds like big and silly talk, but it isn't, it's really a fact. It's neither boasting, nor is it ridiculous, because I know it to be a fact. I get up to give an invocation, and instead of these formal things that you give through your adenoids and your tonsils, something will strike me, and the spark comes, and I let the things come, just let 'em go, of their own accord. I know what I'm saying at the time, and I can stop when I want to stop. It isn't a thing like being in a trance or hypnosis, but it's darn near it. To me God is that something that's everything, that's above us and in us, and in everything.

And I pray to God as I would pray to an individual, because you can't pray to a force, to a general power or something like that. When I pray, I talk *with* God, just like I would talk with you.

And I tell him what I'm thinking, and I ask his strength and help and inspiration to do the thing the way it should be done and also to care for us and to guard us—and this means very much to me. Prayer is a very real thing to me, but when you ask me how it operates, and is it effective, is it going to work, I say I don't know. I don't know. But I do feel an inner strength and power all through my life. Here I am in my eighties, and I feel like sixty. I feel that power within me. And I think it's helped me; it's given me years and strength and the ability to move at least some people, to touch them, and to make their lives a little sweeter and more thoughtful. That's the way I look at God.

SWEENEY: Have there been any major changes in your attitude on God?

MAGNIN: No, I've been that way pretty much since I went to the seminary, the Hebrew Union College in Cincinnati. Even then theology meant nothing to me; God was above theology. Theology is poor philosophy. Philosophy is bad enough. It's nothing but juggling of words, nothing but prestidigitation, you know, whatever they call it. It's a lot of words, and no two philosophers ever agree with each other, so it must be just words. Two physicists agree on the law of gravity as something, two chemists will agree that a certain combination will cause an explosion, or something is poison, but no two philosophers ever agreed, and no two theologians. Maybe that's why there are so many different religious sects. They're all trying to say the same thing but by different routes. They're trying to bolster up their faith by words. But faith is greater than words. I can't explain my faith by mere words. Words are limited. Words are like glasses that contain just so much.

SWEENEY: Have there been any experiences in your life in which you have felt the presence of God in an especially strong way?

MAGNIN: Not in the way that people do who get up and yell and scream, not in that sense. No, except in what I do. I'll sit quietly and meditate sometimes, or when I'm in that pulpit and I'm speaking, or when I invoke the blessing of God. For instance, I was at the Opera Guild the other day, and I was supposed to give an invocation. What do you give them, what do you pray for at an Opera Guild? What do you ask for? That I should become a Caruso? Suddenly the thought struck me: who wrote the first opera, who composed it? What was the name of it? It was called *The Creation*. And there was that great thundering voice, and he did all the electric work. He put all the lights up there, the sun, the moon, the stars; and he wrote the music, music of the spheres, from that to the sound of a cricket, and all the motion of a blade of grass. He did the scenery. He did the acting. He did everything. Greatest opera ever composed. This is the blessing I prayed for—all in two minutes—and people were weeping. And I myself was deeply moved, and I didn't know how it happened. And then they wanted copies. I said, "I can't give you copies, I didn't write that." Does this sound strange to you?

SWEENEY: No. It sounds beautiful. It sounds like, you know, God really does speak. He can speak through human instruments.

MAGNIN: That's my concept of the prophets and great religious teachers, Saint Francis of Assisi, or whoever they are. And I read all of them. To me they all mean something. I've never locked myself up in a closet with a religious label. Wherever beauty comes from, wherever poetry or wisdom comes from, I want to grasp it, I reach out for it—whether Jewish or Christian or whatever.

SWEENEY: The third question. . . .

MAGNIN: I didn't answer the first two!

SWEENEY: Well, sure you did! (laughter) You said regarding the first question that. . . .

MAGNIN: Ah, go ahead!

SWEENEY: . . . that God is beyond knowledge and definition, but you can know him through intuition.

MAGNIN: Yeah, well, what's the third question?

SWEENEY: The third question is, Who are you to God?

MAGNIN: Pardon me?

SWEENEY: Who are you to God? How do you think God looks upon you?

MAGNIN: I don't know. I act and pray as though he really knew about me and could take an interest in me. But just what happens, how do I know? This is faith; that isn't something you can prove. It's a feeling. I don't like the word faith, even; it's a feeling, it's a feeling. Faith is a nice word, but it's been so abused. It's become a dogmatic thing, you see.

SWEENEY: Can you elaborate a little bit on the feeling of God in your life?

MAGNIN: Well, I've always had a feeling that God does know me, love me, and care for me. And when I really think about that, it seems silly that out of the billions who've lived and died he'd love me. See, when you get into logic, it seems impossible. There again, you transcend logic. It's a feeling. I have the feeling that he—and I say *he,* he's not either man nor woman—is really interested in me. And if you ask me to explain this feeling, I can't, of course, nor do I take it too literally. But it's there; maybe it's an illusion I've created for my own comfort—so what's the difference? We use crutches when we can't walk, if you have an accident you use a crutch. What's wrong with a crutch? People criticize religion because it's a crutch, but that's the nicest part of it. When we have an operation, we use an anesthetic. Do we want to do without it and suffer the pain? Religion may be an illusion, an anesthetic, but it's a beautiful one and I'm willing to accept it. I think it's more than that myself, but anyone who says it's just something you want to comfort you, I say that's good enough. I don't apologize for it. I want anything that's going to make life sweeter and happier, there's no question about it. It's short enough as it is.

SWEENEY: Well, anything you want to add in closing?

MAGNIN: No, I want to ask you though—it's nothing to do with this—when'd you decide to become a priest? How old are you now?

SWEENEY: I'm thirty-two.
MAGNIN: I'm eighty-six. You can shut the recorder off. Now let me ask you. . . .

WILLIAM PETER BLATTY

Bill Blatty's novel and screenplay, The Exorcist, *stirred up considerable controversy on diabolical possession and demonic powers. Word has it that Blatty based his story on an actual case of possession, though the child possessed was a boy rather than a girl, and no one died during the exorcism. (As a priest, I have experienced many evil influences, but the most terrifying were not with people tormented by evil and abused by the devil; rather, they were with people who claimed absolute truth was theirs—people who, in the name of divinity, demanded absolute, blind loyalty from others.) The purpose of this interview, however, was not to find out what Bill thought of the devil, but of God.*

BLATTY: Your first question to me was to define my relationship with God. Before I can answer that, let me say that I find myself formulating answers that are in terms of my problems with God. For example, this morning my wife told me that today our six-month-old son would get his first taste of meat. And I immediately said, "That's unfortunate." I began to brood about dog-eat-dog, and that we must seek nutriments from the suffering of living creatures, which they are. I mean they're sentient, conscious, aware of their suffering, as anyone will attest who has heard a dog scream with pain run over by a car. That certainly presents the image of either a very strange God with a cruel or an unfeeling side to his nature, or again thrusts us back to the question of original sin. And I found myself thinking of John Henry Newman's allegory about coming upon a pirate ship and finding aboard among all these barbarous people a young man of apparently very noble lineage, very well-mannered, very generous in his actions, and kind. What questions would this raise? Well, immediately we think, this boy doesn't belong on this ship. There has been somewhere, some terrible, fundamental cleavage between this boy and his family. This is not where he belongs. This is not his natural environment. And that, I think, is accurately the case with us. This is not our natural environment. These problems are susceptible to various explanations with varying degrees of satisfaction. But, on the other hand, I find great mystery, not in the problem of evil but in the problem of good. If we are finally reducible to nothing more than molecular structures, amino acids and so on, goodness is very mysterious. It's very mysterious that one man, being of sound mind, can give his life for another. I think that kind of love, that kind of inherent goodness speaks very loudly for a good God. At one time maybe man was not a meat-eating animal. Did you ever consider original sin as a genetic event? For example, assume that we have come to this point of scientific wisdom and technology before, dropped a few bombs which caused tremendous damage to the earth and everything on it, and created a mutation, a monster, if you will—and we are it. And therefore evolution is a process of reevolving, of reascending to man's state. Quite frankly, I think that is what is happening.

And so with all the problems, I personally have always felt that my relationship to God is that of a son who writes lots of letters. He never gets a letter back, but he keeps hearing reports from mutual friends of what his father is doing. And his father seems to be taking the attitude of "look, trust me, I'm taking care of you." And I do trust him, I trust God very definitely. There have been so many personal interventions in my life. Maybe it's fanciful. Any one event, I suppose, would be fanciful, but take something as simple as, oh, when I was just graduating from grammar school. I desperately wanted a scholarship to Xavier High School—the only way I could get to Xavier was through a scholarship—and I think I spent one entire afternoon saying decades of the rosary; my knees hurt. I did not get the scholarship, I did not go to Xavier, but approximately four years later, when again I didn't have a penny and I wanted to go to Georgetown, I took seven hours of the college board exams, finished them feeling that even if I had money, Georgetown would not accept me. They gave out one scholarship a year. And, lo and behold, while I was working at a summer resort, I got a letter informing me that I was given the scholarship. And it's that kind of intervention that I've felt constantly, constantly, in my life. God, my mysterious father. And somewhere we have gone wrong. And I suppose that there is even more suffering in the world, certainly, than man's spiritual evolution demands. And that's not my father's fault, that's the fault of the race. Someplace we did something like creating monsters—genetic damage.

While we're talking about suffering, it's interesting to wonder whether or not God could—whether through the process of evolution or instant creation—produce humanity without it. Would it be possible to produce a man if there were not even the possibility of suffering? Not even that to reckon with? Wouldn't we simply be on the level of a chess-playing koala bear? In other words, is there any other way to come out with *man*? If we as a potential entity could be quizzed . . . God my father quizzes me in potential and says, "We have these questions: You can be a koala bear. And I'm going to put you in koala bear heaven. You will always have all the eucalyptus leaves you want. You will never feel pain. I'm going to put you in a protective plastic bubble. You will be as content as a koala bear can be. Or I have this strange idea I call man—you know about angels—but there is this . . . 'man,' and it has a body, and there's only one way you can get to that, only one way to achieve that kind of nobility: I have to give you free choice, and I have to put you into the furnace. You're going to suffer, and worse than that, you're going to see the suffering of those who are close to you. And you're going to despair. And even then I cannot guarantee your humanity. But that's your only shot, I mean, that's the way we make men. You want man, that's the only means. Your choice."

I have to imagine that that's the choice I made, that we all made, that Adam made—I want to be a man, I don't want to be a koala bear. Give me the suffering. Too bad I won't know it then, which will increase my suffering, but everything's going to come out in the end.

I don't believe personally that God my father is going to condemn to hell the Neanderthal that I run into now and then on the street, because he's a Neanderthal. At the same time, I cannot imagine a continuation of that Neanderthal's existence after death. What is God's justice for him? What is his mercy for him? What is it? What is his state, since he has never evolved? He has a consciousness, but it is so primitive he wouldn't know God if he fell over him, or happiness, if it hit like a building. And all I can find is that—I'm not talking about reincarnation—it seems to me that this life is one, for some, of many lives. Not necessarily on this planet, not necessarily in any form vaguely resembling the human. I have no idea, none whatever. *But we get to make a choice.* We don't just make choices in life; I think we continue to make choices after death.

SWEENEY: You mentioned a moment ago that you're like a person who writes letters to God. And you really don't get a direct response back, but you are comforted by the fact that there are other people writing letters and getting information.

BLATTY: Sure. It's like going to an island where they say, "Gee, he just checked out of this room a week ago. He was here. Did you see him? Look, there's a book, some papers he left behind."

SWEENEY: So in your experience there has been no intimate experience of God touching you directly, but there have been interventions of God in your life.

BLATTY: Yes. Without a doubt. There's certainly been no mystical experience of God for me. Not even remotely. Unless one would want to include something like what happened when Whitaker Chambers looked at his daughter's ear at the dinner table one night and said, "The atoms didn't come together by chance to form that ear." Just in that way there are moments when God's presence is irrefutable. I mean it is almost self-evident in those moments. There is no need—you cannot prove it—but it is demonstrated in all of nature. I've certainly felt, experienced that. Ever since, well when was the first time I had that experience? During my freshman year at Georgetown, I was standing out on a veranda towards sunset overlooking the Potomac, and the sun was hitting the clouds and the river in a way that . . . one could have only used the word "glorious" to describe it. And I felt filled with an inner radiance. It was certainly an intuitive embrace of God, of God's presence.

SWEENEY: At that moment?
BLATTY: Yes. Intuitively. In that piece of nature I was looking at, I felt God; I mean, it was also a physical sensation. I felt—my chest seemed to fill up, to well up with something wonderful—I feel it now. Yes, I'm feeling it right now. But that's, you know, at the bottom of the ladder leading to mystical experience. I don't think I've been a good enough person to have that direct encounter.

But I must be a favorite child, because he keeps sending me and giving me all these other little clues, and blessings, all along the way. Yeah, I must have . . . how's it put? "Somewhere in my childhood I must have done something good. . . ."
SWEENEY: When you consider God, does it have to do primarily with intuitions and experiences of beauty in nature and people?
BLATTY: I . . . I always have a feeling of God going back to the metaphor of the father, as someone or something in a sense parental. I mean, that's the analogy that for me comes closest to it. Parental, protective; I guess the exact word would be providential. I am in his keeping and care. The lilies of the field. I feel that very, very strongly, maybe because I've been lucky enough to live the Horatio Alger story. So how can I escape feeling that way about God?

When I was a child, right up to the time I started college, we were evicted from wherever we lived, roughly every three months—I think that's the average—for non-payment of rent, and my mother lived like a benevolent, suffering Fagan—a Lebanese Fagan. She had to outwit the landlords. And my father earned seven dollars a week while he lived. He died when I was quite young. And my mother provided for us by begging on the streets. Literally begging. And when I survey my surroundings at the moment, and when I reflect upon my mother's most serene confidence that everything was going to be terrific, not to worry, now I cannot help thinking of God's providence. I cannot help being powerfully impressed by it. He loves me *anyway*. And I don't know what the future holds for me in his plan. Normally, the kind of affluence or ease that I have are not helpful to attaining the Kingdom of God. So maybe there will be a change, although I feel that I'm now free to do a lot of good work that will help a lot of people, and will satisfy, fulfill me.

SWEENEY: Do you have any idea of who you are to God or how God might look upon you?

BLATTY: I think that my answer to that finally is going to be no, that I have no idea. Having said that, I can—what can I do?—I can speculate. I don't mean to wander in pantheism, but maybe in some sense I am a piece of God, one of the electrons in his being. Maybe the closest I can come to it is what I learned in an argument from . . . was it natural theology? Or general ethics? Goodness is diffusive of itself. I believe that to be so. That's the only reason for generosity or kindness—goodness *is*; we see it in the actions of certain men. Then how do we account for it? And if we see that in certain men goodness is diffusive of itself, this certainly reflects the nature of the author of creation. It in some sense reflects an aspect of God's being.

SWEENEY: Do you think your belief in God has any influence on your unconscious, on how you dream and how you write?

BLATTY: What an interesting question. Does my belief in God influence what I dream? I'll start with that.

My suspicion is that it does. Only because of just a general belief of mine, totally unsupported by one shred of evidence, that somehow faith, belief in anything, creates a climate in which certain things can happen that normally do not or would not happen. And so I think my belief in God—and this is extreme speculation—may have something to do with the all too visible interventions in my life, for example, the psychic content, the precognitive content of my dreams.

Does it affect what I write or how I write? What I write, certainly. Because I am drawn to theological themes. I am drawn to give hope to those who have not been as fortunate as I have in the little clues to God's existence and providence. How I write? Well, certainly I tap my unconscious to a tremendous extent when I write. I set the problem for my unconscious, and then after about six weeks of false starts encircling the typewriter, there is a flow, an unremitting flow that doesn't stop. And without a plan or an outline, everything falls into place. I'll never forget, when I was writing the novel *The Exorcist,* I had originally created Burke Dennings, the director, as comic relief. And you cannot

imagine my surprise when I realized he was going to be murdered. I cried out in shock at the typewriter: "My God, Burke
Dennings is going to be killed!" Now, that was absolutely right for
making that particular novel work. I don't know what I would
have done without that. I had no plan, but something planned it.
And that is my unconscious, and my unconscious knows more
than my consciousness knows, as does yours, as does everyone's.
It is a larger personality, maybe *the* primary aspect or reality of
our psyche, and in some way—I'm almost positive, I mean, this is
a very strong opinion of mine—I think the unconscious is the link
to God. I think that's the direct channel, right there. You just open
it up and let it come in. That's the part of us that I think is always in
touch with our Father, and keeps getting reassured, and keeps
saying, "Yes, yes, I see, right, right, it's okay, all right, it's going to
turn out well."

Some psychiatrists have suggested that maybe our sleeping
state is more important than our waking state—that it is reality.
And this is the dream state, although the secondary state. I
certainly couldn't write without my unconscious, without
reliance on my unconscious, consciously tapping my unconscious, telling my unconscious here is the problem, here are the
elements, take over, work it out, would you, and when you've got
it worked out, let me know. And when I am looking peripherally
at the problem, in comes the answer.

SALLY STANFORD

Sally consented to an interview in the midst of a busy evening of managing her Valhalla Restaurant. The former madam was mayor of Sausalito, California, from March of 1976 through March of 1978. She told me she was elected mayor because, instead of sending out fliers with a lot of political mumbo-jumbo, she mailed out valentine cards with "I love you" on them. She was a hearty, outspoken, witty woman. Sally died February 1, 1982. May she rest in peace.

SWEENEY: How long have you been mayor here?

STANFORD: Since last March.

SWEENEY: How do you like it?

STANFORD: Well, I . . . if you had three votes, I'd like it better.

SWEENEY: My questions are very basic ones that focus on your experience. And you can approach the first any way you want: Who is God to you?

STANFORD: Well, I think God is many things to many people. I think God is love and understanding, good will toward your fellow men. I'm not sure if there's some mythical person sitting up there, but there is a higher force. You know that the tides come at a certain moment, and they leave at a certain moment; there's a mathematical pattern of being. And what you send into the lives of others must come back into your own, because that's the pattern of being. So you don't do things to other people that you wouldn't like to have them do to you, because some day you have to face tomorrow.

When you set out to destroy somebody else, eventually you destroy yourself, because you must pay for what you do. Usually when you gain some great facade of respectability, great honor, the house of cards falls apart—you have to pay for what you do. So you should never do things to other people that you don't want to have come back into your own life. It's the old Arabic adage: "Revenge not thyself while sitting on the threshold of thine home. Behold, the corpse of thine enemy passeth." But we've shortened it a little bit, and we say, "When you sit by the crack of the door long enough, you see your enemy go by in a hearse and you never have to get up." 'Cause it's gonna happen to him anyway. That you can depend on.

SWEENEY: Have you ever had what you would consider an experience of God?

STANFORD: Well, I have, everyone has, but they don't develop it, they don't use it. It's extra sensory perception. In the early days people were alert to the rustling of a leaf, the breaking of a twig, because it was self-preservation. And the danger was ripe. I've always had that awareness. I can feel things. I can walk into a room and feel the tempo. Lot of people can't do that, because they never trained their mind to do it; I've had to, and I do. I can walk into a place, and I can know things are wrong; for example, I may say to my restaurant manager here, "There're certain things wrong, here, I want to tell you that." And sure enough, it'll all come to pass. It will all come out in the open.

SWEENEY: So, in terms of this strong sensitivity, you were about to say whether you have had an experience of God.

STANFORD: Yes. I feel that those who have gone before us—it's like when you have a piece of property and you plant some trees against the wind and the rain, and they become your shelter—I think that those who have loved you and passed before you are all there someplace. You know, a protective force for you. I believe that. All I know is that I've had many protective forces around me, and I know there is a higher force.

SWEENEY: Can you describe one or two incidents where that higher force has really stood out?

STANFORD: Yes. Yes. In 1939 something happened, and I got in a lot of trouble. It was in all the papers. And none of my friends came to help me. My mother, who had died two years earlier, came to me in a dream. I'd never dreamt about her before. She said, "Don't worry, you're going to sleep, but first I want to cook you some breakfast. I'll make some hot biscuits, bacon and eggs, and I have some homemade jelly." And she said, "Now, Marcie, that's a meal good enough for anyone. Come on, I want you to eat something." I saw her so plain. And then I went to bed, and she was tucking me in. The next day, Harry Lerner from the *Chronicle*, who owed me nothing, was very kind to me. He straightened out all the trouble.

I think those who love you never leave you. Call it God, or call it whatever you will. No one has ever seen him face to face, but I believe in reincarnation, that nothing ever dies. It changes form a number of times, but it's always there. I think people should be taught, especially young people, to live as best they can because I think that you come back reincarnated into the same sphere you left. You want to stay in the gutter all your life, you can stay there, if you have no ambition to reach. You take a small plant; if you put it in the shadow with the sunlight above it, it'll grow and reach the light. No matter how small it is.

SWEENEY: Has there been an experience where you have felt almost the direct contact or touch of God?

STANFORD: Many times. Once a burglar attacked me, hit me over the head four times with his gun, and threatened to kill me if I screamed. I grabbed the gun, and he ran away.

SWEENEY: Was he caught?

STANFORD: Yeah, they got him. And I've been sick, too, terribly sick. In fact, I've had six major heart attacks.

SWEENEY: Six?

STANFORD: Yes. Six.

SWEENEY: Have you had open heart surgery, or. . . .

STANFORD: Oh, no. None of that. It was suggested, but I wouldn't have it. I wouldn't do it. I believe in mind over matter.

SWEENEY: How long ago was this most recent attack?

STANFORD: Oh, it'll be . . . had one here a year ago, during the elections. Don't remember a thing. Went to the hospital and I pulled out of it. You don't know how you're gonna survive it all. You can't give up because something's happened to you; you have to keep moving.

SWEENEY: Has your attitude toward God changed since you were small?

STANFORD: Well, of course in my early life, my mother was very religious. Not so much my father, but they were always sitting down waitin' for God, you know, to take care of them. I said, well, you have to get out and do a few things yourself. He can't take care of the whole world. You got to get out and get with it. Do the best you can.

My first interpretation of the Bible was when I was five years old. The minister's kids had better shoes than we did, nice black patent leather Mary Jane shoes, and pretty hair ribbons. I had prettier hair than they did, but I wanted to have some of those nice things, too. So I didn't think they needed my nickel in the collection plate, because we needed some bread at home. And then there was this hell and brimstone, and God's going to burn you forever and ever, and destroy you, and all that. I could never get used to the idea that he would be a God of hate and hell.

But I've had many protective forces around me that I've wondered about. Suddenly out of nowhere comes help. That's a strange thing. And I know there's a higher force, whether you call it God, or what the hell you call it. There's somebody up there, watching over you.

SWEENEY: Do you pray to God? Or that force?

STANFORD: Well, I'm not any churchgoer per se. I do what I can, and I say a prayer once in a while, probably not for myself but for others.

SWEENEY: Why won't you pray for yourself?

STANFORD: Well, I don't know. But I have my own religion, if you call it religion. Always like Omar Khayyam when he said in *The Rubáiyát*

There was a door to which I found no key,
There was a veil past which I could not see:
Some little talk awhile of me and thee
There seemed—and then no more of thee and me.

SWEENEY: Is that the poem that best describes your religion?

STANFORD: Well, probably not. I believe in reincarnation. I believe that nothing ever dies. It changes form many times. It's like the Indians feel they must give their dead back to the earth. That's why they wrap them in cloth and put them in the earth.

They must put back into the earth what they've taken from the earth.

SWEENEY: Suppose there was a ten- or eleven-year-old child here, and she asked, "What's God mean to you?" How would you respond to that?

STANFORD: I'd tell her God is love and understanding.

SWEENEY: How would you describe yourself?

STANFORD: Just myself? It's kind of hard for me to describe myself. Everybody thinks they know all about you, and they really don't know anything about you, really, your secret heart. What makes you tick.

SWEENEY: What makes you tick?

STANFORD: I don't know. I wonder sometimes. Have you wondered, too, about yourself?

SWEENEY: Yes. Have you come close to an answer? You must have come up with one or two. You've had a long time to try at it.

STANFORD: Well, I just try to do what I can for others. You can't take on the whole world, but you do what you can. And you didn't bring a damn thing into it, and you're not going to take it with you, anyway. So you might as well do something for others, if you can, and help them.

Here's a poem that says a lot about how I feel. It's called "My Creed." It's anonymous, as far as I know.

I do not choose to be a common man.
It is my right to be uncommon, if I can.
I seek opportunity, not security.
I do not wish to be a kept citizen,
Humbled and dulled by having the state look after
    me.
I want to take the calculated risk,
To dream, to build, to fail, and to succeed.
I refuse to barter incentive for a dole.
I prefer the challenges of life to the guaranteed
    existence,
the thrill of fulfillment to the stale calm of Utopia.
I will not trade freedom for benefice,
not my dignity for a handout.
It is my heritage to think and act for myself,

Enjoy the benefits of my creations, and to face
The world boldly, and say, this I have done.
All this is what it means to be an American.
And here's one last one that I've used many times in passing:
Rage on, rage on, O mortal storm;
I love your wicked soul. Unleash the lightning,
    unleash the flood,
Let the thunder roll.
Mow down the cringing weakling, let him moan
    and cry and pray.
Alone I'll fish your fury and I'll dance to what you
    play.

EUGENE MCCARTHY

A former university professor and author of more than a dozen books, he served as a United States representative and senator from Minnesota from 1949 to 1970.

MCCARTHY: To the third question, Who am I to God? I could use the Chesterton quotation: "God knows." I think the first time I ever used this answer as a form of defense was on the campus of Berkeley. It was just one of those things—someone back in the crowd asked: "Do you believe in God?" This is the kind of question that interrupts a political interview. David Frost asked me that in the middle of an interview, which was silly. It's like Barbara Walters playing games. Both times I was saved by Chesterton. I gave them his answer and left it at that. How do you want me to proceed, with the first question?

SWEENEY: Yes. Who or what is God to you?

MCCARTHY: I suppose everyone says it's a hard question. I would not really define it—it's a little like the idea of music minus one, where you sort of leave out the melody and build all around it. When you're done, you're sensitive to what you don't know, or to what's missing. That, in a way, is the negative concept—what you have left when you can't explain anything other than by some concept or acceptance of God as a reality. In a way, it's the negative of the traditional theological explanation of the degrees of being. From that approach I think that Chardin had part of the understanding of it as a kind of Becoming—not really evolution, but something more intense than that. Not in a sort of sequential or temporal order. I guess that's about what it is. And if it's a reality, then ultimately it has to be, probably has to be personal. Is that enough on that?

SWEENEY: Yes, if you wish. Concerning the second question: How has your relationship with God. . . .

MCCARTHY: I suppose what you mean is a kind of experience—not really full understanding, but short of that. I just happened upon one of Yeats' poems—I don't recall which one it is—but he says something like: My fiftieth year has come and gone, and I sit a solitary man in a crowded London shop, with open book and empty cup upon the marble table top. But while on the street shop I gazed, my body of a sudden blazed, and for twenty minutes more or less, I felt such happiness, that I felt that I was blessed and could bless.

I don't know—maybe most of us have two or three experiences of that kind, not really transcendence, it's just an "intensity," a "fullness," which Yeats described in the above poem. I'd say maybe two or three times in my life under various circumstances I had a sense of this—whether it was intimacy or something else. And about two times this "intensity" happened in relation to nature, along the line expressed by Keats' "On First Looking into Chapman's Homer"—a sort of spirituality of nature.

And I think once or twice since I've been in the pursuit of knowledge there has been an enlightenment, both in a kind of "unity" and "otherness." Do you know who wrote the book *The Psychology of Mystics*?

SWEENEY: No.

MCCARTHY: It was that sort of experience, a special kind of insight, which you can't really explain in terms of just the normal pursuit. One author describes this in his theology of hope, that level where there is really nothing left but hope. And that means that you are trying in some way to speak about your close kind of experience of God.

I suppose the third kind of "God experience" might be something of just a personal relationship, like looking at sleeping children, where you sense that it's not just you and they, but something more. I'd say those are probably the three general areas where I've experienced God. If you asked which was a particular experience, I'd say that's pretty hard to say—it would be like trying to remember what Ronald Reagan said—it happened but I don't remember what it was.

I might add, though it has not been a deep experience, the experience of music. I had a metaphysics professor, a Benedictine monk who said he was persuaded that the only communication eventually would be music, and that this was what it was all about. I got a foretaste of it in certain moments when the musical experience was rather complete.

I wrote this poem called the "Aardvark," and I guess it's a metaphor, I don't know. I've said that the proper study of mankind is really animals. You have to understand them before you can understand human relations. A metaphor is something you use to explain something that is more difficult to understand. The aardvark so far as I know didn't evolve from anything, and it isn't evolving into anything. So it is kind of an absolute metaphor: you can say the aardvark is like any other animal, but you can't say any other animal is like the aardvark, because if it is, it is an aardvark. Similarly, we can say God is like Fr. Sweeney in some respect, but you can't say Sweeney is like God, because if he is, he is God. This is an oversimplification, but I think it is in this kind of range that I have to respond to this question.

SWEENEY: So you mentioned some of this sense of transcendence, in terms of nature, in terms of knowledge, in terms of personalities. . . .

MCCARTHY: And music, in tribute to Fr. Ernest Kilzer's thesis. It could be music, or it could be some other artistic experience. Music was primarily what he saw. And I think he's right.

SWEENEY: In your response to question one, a description you gave of God was one who is "becoming," in the Chardinian sense. Did I hear that correctly?

MCCARTHY: Well, I should have said that is what creation is about, a sort of becoming, but that God is absolute, ultimate, rather than something you try to measure in time or whatever. (Only Walter Cronkite can control time once you've got it started. Even God couldn't interfere with time he started. Television—you can classify it, reverse it, do with it whatever you want.)

SWEENEY: I'd like to zero in on the "person" or "personality" aspect of your understanding of God. In traditional Christian theology there is a presentation of experiencing God through the person of Jesus. In your descriptions you didn't talk about any of that. . . .

MCCARTHY: Except in reference to an "absolute metaphor." You can say that God in some respects is like Jesus, but it's hard to say the reverse, because you're talking about a being which we don't understand. (Unless, as I said, if Fr. Sweeney is God, then the metaphor is fulfilled—and we're not sure of that.)

SWEENEY: At moments in your life when you did experience this deeper sense, was there an individuality to this deeper sense? Obviously, when you experience something in nature, there is individuality all around you. . . .

MCCARTHY: Yes, I think two things: there is a kind of separation, but also a kind of identification with person or being—if you're talking about being, about person in some sense. We don't know quite what "person" is. . . . So, that's about it. . . .

SWEENEY: One last question: Do you have a sense that you are communicating with this being, this God?

MCCARTHY: I don't know whether it's communication, or whether it just sort of happens at the same time, a directed sort of thing. I just sort of see God in the whole creation, as Chardin speaks of it. And as I mentioned in my interview for the Eugene Kennedy book *Believing*: If God had just one doubt, he'd try not to be, or just allow non-being, which then would have to build back until there was a full identification. I think that one has an obligation to try to understand nature, persons, music, and the intellectual thrust—and that this is, in a way, an act of worship. It's what worship is all about. And if you have any talents, to try to communicate to other people—this is what art's about. Yeats said it: the function of art is "To bare the soul of man to God." The "profane perfection" of mankind is from poetic insights.

JEREMY HOLLINGER

What Mother Teresa does in Calcutta, Brother Jeremy does on skid row in Los Angeles. He serves the "poorest of the poor." His vocation as a Missionary of Charity is to be a loving presence in the midst of people despised and rejected. He has a quiet, extremely peaceful bearing.

HOLLINGER: I couldn't begin to tell you who God is except as I've known him personally. I guess, basically, it's a very simple type of thing: knowing him as a friend, as someone intensely concerned about me as a person. As I thought about your question, all the words that kept coming back to describe God were the sort of words you would use to describe a relationship of love. God is someone who cares enough to be concerned about the day-to-day things that are happening in my life and has a part, not in determining what they are, but in directing them. God is a very personal, loving friend.

And yet, the word friend doesn't really describe God, because when I pray I find the word Father is the most natural way to describe this other person, this relationship. I like to reflect a little on Isaiah, about how God has watched over you while you were in the womb, how he has formed you in his hand, and taken you from the road. It's that sort of image of father and child, of being led along the way.

In school you are taught that God is all-knowing and all-loving, but the definitions can never really replace *knowing that you are loved.* When you ask, Who am I to God? again, it would be that relationship of a person loved, and because of that, able to love other people. To be loved by God, to know that he really cares what happens, no matter how awful I may feel, or what a mess I've made of my life. It's sort of knowing that you are never going to be alone, that there's always something deeper, there's always this one person in your life who's not going to abandon you. All other friends can fail you at times, or let you down, or not be there when you need them, but God is there. I really believe that. He's watched over me thus far, he's formed me, and he's still doing that. That's very special. It's amazing. In fact, sometimes it's almost overwhelming.

I used to think that with God you sort of had to sit down and talk to him, tell him where you were. I find more and more that really isn't necessary. He sort of knows. It's a sense almost of a daily being with this loving person. Because he loves you, you just have to love him in return. For me, there's no other way to think of it.

I especially reject and am turned off by the kind of serious God I felt was presented when I was younger—this God who couldn't laugh. As I'm coming to know God more deeply, I'm finding he is joyful, laughing, full of mirth—so concerned, and yet able to laugh at what we do, which is often so . . . crazy. To see us as we are in all honesty, and yet just to love us. And I think of this laughing God—not a mocking God, not a jeering God, nothing like that—as a person overwhelmed with exuberance, life, love. God is caring, trusting, joyous.

And yet, I guess part of the experience I've had, especially in the last year or two, has been that I've known God when he wasn't as close, it seemed, or at a time when *I* wasn't joyful. I was feeling a lot of pain, but that's part of the relationship too. I've been asked to do things I would not choose to do. And it's not as if God comes down, sits in this room, and says: "O.K., this is what you have to do next week." Rather, it's a sort of awareness that your life is being directed in this way; and that means there's going to be some things that are painful, and he seems to ask more of that at times than at others. It's sort of been—I like Dorothy Day's words—that "harsh and dreadful" kind of love. It hasn't been all sweet and joyful. It hasn't all been apple pie. At times it's been pretty gruesome. And I find the only way I can approach God at times is just to be angry. You know, really lay it on the line, demand to know why this is happening. That's my own insecurities, of course, yet I know the whole time I'm angry and upset he's still going to be there. That he'll sort of roll with that punch, laugh at it. And we'll get through it somehow.

There's not much structure to my relationship with God. The only thing I can say with certainty is there's a presence. And that presence I feel at different times. Sometimes I go into the chapel here when it's dark . . . and silent. I just listen to the silence. Listen to the heart. Sometimes God is really present in the most outrageous places, downtown on the streets, or on the most noisy and crowded buses—the last places you'd expect God to be. Like when I was going to college, I'd experience God's presence in a dance, in the midst of rock music, which is supposed to dash all solitude and silence. And yet, God was there too.

God's just there. And in people. Meeting him in silence, meeting him in nature, in the beauty around me, just seeing him here. I look out this window and see the city lights; just that can bring me in touch with God. But especially in people: You keep coming back to that beauty in people, which you realize has a much deeper source. When you see how people suffer, and you see how they still believe in people, they still trust, and they still love even though they've been hurt and crushed. You know, I have to believe God's there.

I've had some pretty dramatic things happen, in trying to comprehend Jesus Christ's suffering. I saw a woman in a hospital bed, ready to die, and yet she was hooked up to all her life machines to keep her body functioning. She literally had her arms stretched out like a cross. And the minute I went into the room the mental picture I got was: *this is Jesus crucified.* He was there in that suffering. It was a modern day cross. Definitely, God was there in that person.

When you have this God who is so loving and giving, you can't help but be touched by that, to be overwhelmed with his generosity, and to want others to know him better. And because I've felt that touch, that love, that affects, I hope, the way I look at others. I've noticed when I've had an experience of encountering God in someone in a very loving way and then go back to the people I live with—the everyday people I sort of take for granted—I can see them in a new way, with new eyes.

I think that's what God is doing to me, he's changing me. I know personally what I was five or six years ago; I know what I am today, to a certain extent. We can never be sure we are not deceiving ourselves, but I think I can be sure there has been a transformation. And that change has helped me to open up. I guess God is to be open to people, to love people without putting labels on them or asking them to be something they're not.

I don't feel I've reached a point where I have it all pat and settled, not at all. I feel like I'm continually growing. It's a continual thing, coming to know God, and the many different things he means to me: the God of silence, the God of gentle breezes, the God in people, in nature, in pain, in loneliness. And I think that's what makes our friendship worth something. Somehow it has gone through the initial stages. You know, when you first meet a person, when you first come to know him, your relationship is pretty rosy, things go well; but then, you get through that, and you go through deeper things of being angry, of not understanding each other, and yet still accepting him later, still loving the person. That's sort of the way I feel God and I work through life.

At different times you could ask me this same question, and I'll be feeling a different way. At this point I've been feeling very peaceful, very joyful.

SWEENEY: In terms of your entire life, have there been any profound experiences of God that have caused a major shift in your attitude toward him?

HOLLINGER: I guess the one basic thing that has changed was my idea of God as a kind of task master, a God who was judging me, almost a God who couldn't forgive. I feel there has been a major shift in that. Now I realize God loves me as a sinner, not as some perfect person I wanted to keep trying to be. Once I realized that he loves sinners, a lot started to happen to me. Before that, the whole emphasis was on what I could do to make God love me, or to make sure I got a place with God in heaven. And I had to really work at that. I guess the major shift has been the realization of how little control I have over that. How much it's been a gift. The most I can do is just sort of say *yes.* And I don't think this change happened at any one time; it's been a continuing thing of just realizing the depths of sinfulness I could go to, of not loving, of how miserable I could be and realizing that even with all of that he still loves me. And he's going to be there. That relaxed relationship. I didn't have to do that much any more—in the legal sense—I didn't have quotas. God wasn't a judge, noticing how I went to Mass, how often I prayed. My whole concept of the relationship now is more of just being with him. I can't get into the legal God anymore; it has no meaning for me.

I think the moment I felt his presence the strongest was in responding to the call to follow him. I read Scripture about how Jesus called the apostles. That must have been a great thing for those twelve men to have experienced this big call, to really feel it deeply, and to know it with such certainty that they could go and do anything without worrying about it. At least in one major time in my life I felt that call. In my case, I had to leave everything I knew, my family, my friends, religious order—in the middle of school—and go to a country at war that I never particularly wanted to go to. And yet somehow I knew that I had to. It's just that certainty. And there's no way to explain that to people. I remember at the time trying to tell people I knew I had to do this. I had to say yes. And I couldn't prove it to them, or explain it to them. Except that through many months of just listening, it became real.

I think that's changed my whole attitude to God, too. I feel more and more I can let him do his thing. I can take time. *I* don't have to get the whole thing together, do this remarkable feat for God, bring his word to everyone, make him known in the world. I can just keep saying yes to what he presents and do that patiently. I'm not normally a patient person; I like to get things done; I like to know what's happening; I like to get them organized. This other is sort of against my own nature, yet more and more I just can't rush it. I feel strongly that when the time is right I'll know what to do, where to go, what path to follow. It kind of amazes me how God keeps doing that to us throughout our lives. It's never a one time thing. We're never called just once to give; it's a constant, deep call. Maybe in ten years I'll have to go in another whole direction. I don't know. I realize I just have to be open.

And that really frees you. You don't have to worry. You can let things happen which look like they're the end of the world for you—totally opposed to everything you've known—and *not* to worry about it.

SWEENEY: There was a comment you made earlier I did not understand. You said, when you were "called" you *left* a religious order?

HOLLINGER: Yes, the Christian Brothers. I had felt called in some vague way when I was in high school. I had read this book about Mother Teresa, and I was attracted to her community. I wrote to them, but never heard from them. So I joined the Christian Brothers. I met them, liked them, and now I see how important that was, because I spent three very important years with them. Without the preparation of those years I could never have followed my next call, which was to leave the Christian Brothers and go to Vietnam to join the Missionaries of Charity. I guess that's how I see my whole life thus far: it's been this series of being prepared, and then taking the next step. And at times, especially this time of leaving the Christian Brothers, of being able to do that, knowing there were a lot of things I was not going to like, that I was afraid of.

For instance, I didn't want to go to Vietnam. I was afraid I'd get over there and not like it, and like the fool come 6,000 miles back, and everyone would say, "Aha, you were just off on a lark again. It's all sort of foolish isn't it?" And yet there were these two things at the time that told me it was good and I had to do it. And they were that, even though I worried at times and was afraid, I felt *at peace,* a very deep feeling that this was what should happen. And also I felt very *joyful.* Those two things have been the criteria I've used ever since then in trying to judge what God keeps asking of me.

I'm sorta frightened of the whole prospect—it's not well ordered, it's not tidy. It's very mysterious in a lot of ways; it keeps leading you on to things you never thought you'd do, to things you're not qualified to do, things you don't have natural inclinations to do. And yet, if you're doing something just because you're talented, what does that say about God? I've always felt when he has to make up for something you're lacking, he can get some of the credit he deserves. A lot of times I feel like he can't be asking this. Why is he doing it? And yet I know somewhere there's a reason.

SWEENEY: So you went to Vietnam to join the Missionaries of Charity?

HOLLINGER: Yes, it's a new religious community.

SWEENEY: Wasn't it started in India?

HOLLINGER: Yes, but their only house outside of India was in Vietnam, and the Americans and Europeans couldn't go to India to join because of government visa problems and that sort of thing. I was told in the summer of that year they would be opening a house in New York, and I could go there. And I was all geared for that. In February I got a letter saying that they couldn't open a house there, that I had to come to Vietnam. So the bottom fell out of my whole plan—that's the way I felt. The minute I read that letter it was like, God, this is the time to have a nervous breakdown! And yet I knew I was going to say yes. Many times after that I doubted. I felt, you know, this can't be it; what's he want me there for? Here I was studying history, and I wondered what a history major can do. I don't have any medical skills. I have no great facility for languages. I didn't have any of the things I felt someone should have if they're going to be called to Vietnam and really do something there.

Well, that sort of thinking was all shot to pieces. I realized God was going to do what he wanted to do.

SWEENEY: How long were you in Vietnam?

HOLLINGER: A year.

SWEENEY: While you were there, you were working with the Vietnamese?

HOLLINGER: Yes. We had very poor, small children, who were living on the streets. In our house during the day over a hundred children were eating and going to school. And at night, about sixty slept there, maybe twenty of them pregnant women who had been living on the street.

We were so unqualified—we were the last people who should have been doing that work. I mean, there should have been a group of sisters or someone there, and yet no one was doing this. It seemed we were called there. People kept coming, in need, and we couldn't ignore that.

SWEENEY: But you couldn't speak Vietnamese?

HOLLINGER: At the beginning, no. Even at the end, the amount I could speak wasn't much. Again, God provided people—Vietnamese women who had known GI's, who I think were prostitutes, and they spoke enough English. With the English and the French and the Vietnamese, we all got along. Talk about trusting in God—O, Lord! We were really living in what was the underground of Saigon. It was a very rough neigborhood; there weren't any foreigners living there. And there we were in the midst of that. Here again, I believe we weren't there for any sort of social work. What really could we do the last years in Vietnam? The tragedy was happening every day. I think it was more of seeing ourselves as a community, called just to be a loving presence there to show that people loved each other in the midst of this strife, the war, and the poverty and ugliness. We figured if we could do that, the other things would fall into place. And they did. . . . And then we had to leave Vietnam.
SWEENEY: What year was this?
HOLLINGER: '74-'75. And then we went to India and made our vows to the community.

After that, we were assigned to come to the U.S., to start a house here. And when you look at that, how absurd the whole thing was in worldly terms! There were five of us, besides our superior, who were the only non-Indians in the community. We'd just made our vows, and we were supposed to go around the world and start our work. And there I think you have to believe that God is a humorous God, that he sets up these situations in which, if you have a sense of humor, you'll just roll on the floor laughing. He sent five of us to Los Angeles. And I felt the joke of all jokes was that I was asked to be the Servant of our community, which, just so you know, means the superior. And I was the youngest one. And you know, you could never really get high on that thought because it was just so ridiculous. Anyone who knew the whole situation must have thought it was a Mickey Mouse show.

So, we've had a lot of time to laugh. For God just to be present, to do things we never expected! And I feel like he's doing that again in my life with this Servant thing. Every now and then, you just feel like saying: "Why don't you go away and leave me alone for a little bit?" You can really be familiar with God. You can really tell him—he won't be insulted—at least I don't believe he would.

You know, if you're looking for a cover for your book, have a picture of Jesus smiling or laughing. I really believe that's the way God is—just filled with laughter and joy.

JERZY KOSINSKI

*Author of *The Painted Bird*, *Being There* (both novel and screenplay), and numerous other books and articles, Jerzy Kosinski was born in Poland. During World War II, the Nazis murdered his grandparents, uncles, cousins, and six million other Jews. He was separated from his parents at the age of six, and had to survive war-torn Poland on his own.*

KOSINSKI: Until the age of six, I recall only physical—at best situational—events all stemming from my relationships with my parents or other children. Also, only behavioral not spiritual guidelines: how to be kind, how to recite poems, how to share my toys with other children, that's all. The actual confrontation with the notion of the Self—of who am I—other than as a physical being—came about during the 1939-1945 war.

At that time, away from my parents, I stayed with various peasant families—all of them Catholic; also, I had gone with all their children through the parish religious schooling in preparation for my First Communion. And so, the first religious truths came to me directly and indirectly from the Catholic Church. And even though I assumed that all this made me a Catholic, one particular dimension set me apart from other boys: I was the only one among them who was circumcised—and I was told that this made me a Jew. I assumed that the circumcision was a proof of commitment for which I could not be directly responsible, since I did not circumcise myself. Nor could I answer to myself—and I prayed to God nobody would ask—when or why or by whom was I circumcised. All I knew was that during the war with the Nazis and the anti-Semites who were hunting the few remaining Jews, my circumcision set me apart—and could lead to my death.

Thus, throughout the war, my Jewishness remained a mystery I tried to but could not resolve. In a curious and ironic way, it was only my physical circumcision that, isolated as I was at the time, led me to assume I was a Jew. And beyond circumcision I had no idea what being Jewish meant. Going to confession, I never confessed to being circumcised or Jewish, since I assumed my being Jewish was obviously no secret to God, who might even have been responsible for it in some way. Also I was afraid that as a mortal, if tortured by the Nazis, my Father Confessor might involuntarily reveal my identity. In sum, throughout the war my Jewishness was never discussed: I saw myself as a "circumcised Catholic." After the war, in the orphanage, when asked what was my religion, I wrote (I could not speak): I am a circumcised Catholic. After I was reunited with my parents, I returned to the Judaic tradition. In time, my father told me that, as a Jew, I must answer the questions: *Who am I? Where did I come from?* and *Where am I going?* And he left it at that. To answer these questions I began to study the Judaic faith. And this was, very briefly, my early religious profile.

SWEENEY: In addition to the religious profile, did you as a boy or young man have any internal experience of God?

KOSINSKI: Of man, not of God. I had always assumed that any attempt at my contact with God would be not only presumptuous, but actually contradictory: since, obviously, if I am his creation, then I experience God through the gift of life, and my obligation is to take care of the gift. The giver, presumably, delivered the gift, or sent the gift, or I inherited the gift from him. Present in the gift, the giver remains nevertheless outside of it, beyond my comprehension. To separate the giver from the gift is, perhaps, to diminish the gift. It is this miracle of life and the supreme mystery of being that unites me with my fellow beings; any speculation about the miracle and mystery of the Supreme Being tends to separate me from them. That is how I have looked at it as a boy, and, frankly, I still look at it that way.

SWEENEY: So you don't have, to your knowledge or awareness, any interior sense of God relating to you?

KOSINSKI: I would consider this to be an inappropriate question.

SWEENEY: Why?

KOSINSKI: Since meeting the creator through the act of my existence, I'm more than conscious of the spiritual aspects of the act of life and the act of my faith in it. . . .

SWEENEY: And it terminates with that act?

KOSINSKI: It does: *"I'm fearfully and wonderfully made"* says the Psalmist (139.14). That's the most appropriate and proper dimension, since my faith in the spiritual purpose of existence presupposes *a priori* and *a posteriori* my meeting with the forces of creation; the only meeting of which I think myself capable, of which I was created to be capable.

SWEENEY: And what is your reflection on people, in particular, the mystics who have claimed knowledge and awareness of God?

KOSINSKI: Any manifestation of life and of faith is sacred; I would never dispute what they think about themselves, about their relationship with society, and about God. While I accept that others meet life and God on different levels, I remain responsible for *one* particular life—mine—which was delivered to me (I might respectfully point out) "individually." That's why I have to tend to it individually, by myself, alone, in the privacy of my inner sanctum, and accord life *around me* the same respect which I pay to life *within me.* For me, any comment upon anyone else's religious beliefs is spiritually inappropriate. I'm a missionary to only *one* particular life: the life within me; and I proselytize only one faith: my faith in the sanctity of life. I refuse to pass judgments on the religious beliefs of others.

SWEENEY: Both in the Catholic and Jewish traditions, there is a very strong traditional notion of "prayer," which supposedly is the individual's way of trying to contact the creator, or God. Now, in light of what you just said . . .

KOSINSKI: My prayer is my exaltation in life's moment; it comes to me moment by moment, always concurrent with the act of life and it's the sole way in which I acknowledge what's spiritual in my existence. I consciously narrow my life to the acts of my faith in it—acts which are spiritually significant—and I keep setting aside anything which is insignificant, which obstructs my awe of creation. This is my prayer; other prayers are creations of others and I look at them the way I look at religions, books, poems, works of art—they are all manifestations of spiritual life. In my life and *for* my life, I have chosen one particular form of spiritual worship, and I manifest it as I go along.

SWEENEY: This is all very fascinating to me—please understand why I am asking these questions . . .

KOSINSKI: By all means, keep asking. You are trying to get as close as possible to what I think—and so do I.

SWEENEY: So, if you were to start a typical day, you'd wake up in the morning, and you'd look at the things that are facing you in the terms of that day . . .

KOSINSKI: I commence my day by facing the one who is facing me: my Self. That confrontation is an act of faith: a prayer of acknowledgment, of gratitude, of exaltation. It is also a moment of awareness that life is not permanent; its gift is a spiritual lease, which might be terminated at any time.

SWEENEY: If you found yourself stuck let's say in terms of writing or some other important . . .

KOSINSKI: I am, above all, a spiritual being: As long as I'm spiritually alive I can't be stuck. The intellectual, social, sexual, physical concerns are secondary, particularly when, through vanity, competition, false notions of achievement, etc., they obstruct the spiritual in me. When they do, they are sins.

SWEENEY: If you find that something is threatening your life, whether it was as a young child in the war, and you feared that somebody might hurt you, or you find that there is something you want very much that you're not getting, what do you do?

KOSINSKI: I think of such fears and wants as obstructions of life—of deprecating the worth of me as a man. To counteract them, I remain grateful for what I have—my life and my awareness of its ·spectacle—rather than fearful of what might happen, regretful of what I don't have or what pains me. Perception of pain has always contributed to my awareness of myself. Sin is allowing pain—any pain—to damage the sanctity of life, to regress the drama of my spiritual redemption.

SWEENEY: And if you see that there is something that is threatening your happiness or your existence, what do you do to overcome that?

KOSINSKI: If it's a threat from within—if it's a threat by vanity for instance, or hurt ego, I confess to the sin of it. Then I analyze it, and I try to ban it, since, clearly, it clouds life, and, filtering the experience and awareness, it diminishes the joy of being alive. If, on the other hand, the threat comes from society—from, say, society's view of me or of my work—I try to disregard it, since I am not responsible for society. It's merely *being there*. If it's a specific physical threat—violence, for instance—I try to save my life, but never by combat. Rather, by hands off—though no hand up; to me, life is shelter, not combat.

SWEENEY: As far as "life being a gift"—do you have any concept or notion as to whether a Being gives that gift of life?

KOSINSKI: An inappropriate question . . .

SWEENEY: Would you explain why that is inappropriate?

KOSINSKI: Because, to me, the spiritual is already vested in the gift of life. For me to pursue the giver is to detract from the gift itself. The gift of life was left at my doorstep of my being, and the giver left it *without* leaving a calling card, that is without making the visit manifest. Entrusted with the gift of spiritual creation, I must remain faithful to it and enhance it by my conduct for as long as it remains in my hands. For me, any attempt at "chasing" the giver, is *ipso facto* turning away from the gift.

SWEENEY: If I were to bring this analogy of the gift and the giver into the ordinary household at the time of Christmas: The family members all exchange gifts. If, after the exchange of gifts, what happened in that family household was what you described (namely, there is no turning from the gift to the person who gave the gift) . . .

KOSINSKI: To me, the giver is implicit in the gift.

SWEENEY: Right, but I would consider it a very unusual household.

KOSINSKI: Life is a very unusual household.

SWEENEY: Absolutely. So, what you're saying is that the gift of life is so comprehensive and overwhelming to human consciousness and awareness that . . .

KOSINSKI: . . . that it incorporates in it the notion of the creation.

SWEENEY: And for you as a human person to try to go beyond that gift is really presumptuous.

KOSINSKI: It would be a sin, since to go beyond the gift is to detract from it—to run away from it.

SWEENEY: It would be a great sin because . . . ?

KOSINSKI: Because I would dare to assume that as a mere human being I have a right to question the nature of the giver; to go beyond the spiritual vested at the creation in the gift of life: the greatest gift there is.

SWEENEY: Then how does this notion carry you to death? And what happens beyond death?

KOSINSKI: Death is the withdrawal of that gift.

SWEENEY: And is that the end? So life terminates, you're dead. Is that the end of that gift?

KOSINSKI: For me to speculate what takes place when life ends is, again, to go beyond the gift, to detract from the greatness and the sanctity of the gift—and of the giver.

SWEENEY: So, you feel it is sinful for you to ask questions as to what may or may not happen to you beyond your death?

KOSINSKI: Of course.

SWEENEY: That's fascinating . . .

KOSINSKI: Well, that's how I was taught by life . . .

SWEENEY: But you were raised in both the Judeo and Catholic traditions . . .

KOSINSKI: Almost everything I have said so far I have felt after the war—both as a Jew and as a circumcised Catholic, so to speak. This was my spiritual inheritance, for which, perhaps, the Catholic Church was a great deal responsible since the issue of the gift of life, and of sin against it, came again and again in my confessions. In a way, all my novels are confessional, confessing to the reader the sins of the protagonist—and *maybe* of the author. They are also nonjudgmental: morally open ended, they encourage the reader to judge what, to him or her, is right or wrong. My attitude towards life carried me spiritually undamaged through the years I lived in Poland under the Communist system. Because of how I felt about life, the party couldn't do anything which could wreck me morally. *They* could never enter the kingdom of heaven within me—"the kingdom of heaven" is the gift of life. Ever since I emerged from the "kindergarten" of World War II, I've refused to commit my spiritual being to anything but life itself. I will not commit it to bureaucracy; I will not commit it to political power; I will not commit it to any institution, association, or group

which combats life or tries to institutionally modify the beliefs
and attitudes of others, or passing socially binding judgments.
Hence, for me, the calling of a novelist is an appropriate one;
fiction is a suspension of disbelief—not a statement of belief; and
since it deals in imaginary situations, it cannot slander or damage
or seduce or convert anyone; it is in no way a "how-to." It tells a
tale but it says nothing. As a novelist, I'm the furthest removed
from being a missionary to any particular faith and to any particular church.

SWEENEY: I think I am missing something. You were raised in
three different traditions: Jewish, Catholic, and Protestant. These
traditions have a very strong emphasis on death being overcome
by a redeemer, salvation, and so on. And sin being overcome. But
somewhere in your own growth, you felt that those questions that
talked about death and eternal life and so on were presumptuous.

KOSINSKI: Yes, because I feel that they could turn away from the
gift of life—from the spirituality and faith already vested in the act
of being.

SWEENEY: Can you hone in on what experience it was in your life
that enabled you to make that break with your own religious
background?

KOSINSKI: Maybe it was the Holocaust which turned me towards
life and exaltation in its gift; during the war I saw life destroyed—
brutally taken away. I saw the frailty of man, both physical and
spiritual. I recognized once and for all that if a human being—a
creature so small, so frail, so short-lasting—is endowed with life,
with such a generous gift, and still thinks it's not enough and
wants to know what happens in the afterlife—well, that's a sin.

SWEENEY: Now I understand. Thank you, that really clarifies it
for me.

KOSINSKI: . . . though until now it has never occurred to me that
I could clarify it for anyone but myself.

SWEENEY: This answers very well the questions that I wanted to
pose. Is there any area of substance or significance in terms of
God . . .

KOSINSKI: I really can't think of anything, other than to say that
what I've said is not based on any system of belief. It is merely
what I feel when I confront myself on waking up. It is my private

faith. In fact, I feel a bit guilty about sharing it with you since I haven't really done it directly—only indirectly and open-endedly through my fiction. I always guard myself against talking about my faith, since talking about it is, however vaguely, a way of proposing it as an outlook, while it is my "in-look." It is something not meant to be discussed; I wake up to my faith in life and my faith in life wakes me up. I would never catalogue it.

SWEENEY: Obviously, you are not trying to proselytize.

KOSINSKI: Never. I am merely talking philosophically—without being philosophical. And with a clear understanding that these are my speculations about my inner state.

SWEENEY: Well, I'm very grateful that you're doing this, because it's presented a point of view that I've never even reflected on before. And I think that there are other people who have not really reflected on this precise point of view or experience. And that, to me, is the value of what you've just done. That you have, through your own reflections on where you are, presented an experience and point of view that may be very unusual, very different.

KOSINSKI: While we all survive on our own, I suspect that a great number of people of my generation share with me—as I do with them—this notion of life as a gift, as the greatest gift there is. *"What is man, that Thou dost make so much of him"* (Job 7:17). Maybe the notion was born during the war so deadly to life . . . or maybe in the aftermath of war, by living under the soulless Communist system. . . .

SWEENEY: That's very clear. Thank you.

HESTER GLORY STORM

Hester was a poet and former Communist. She suf-
fered considerably from cancer, and in the midst of
this, according to her closest friend, achieved an inner
peace and a profound level of mysticism. She died
August 1, 1979. May she rest in peace.

SWEENEY: If I recall, you said that God is the maker of everything and the lover of everything.

STORM: That's a very short, quick answer. God is the beauty of everything.

SWEENEY: In a lot of your poetry you talk about your longing for God and the comfort you take in the life Jesus led. Before we began to tape you were mentioning the experience of your operation for cancer a year ago. And you said that immediately before you were taken into the operating room, Fr. Don Merrifield, a good friend of yours, told you that he was going into the chapel to pray for you and that you were going to be with the Lord. And from that time on, if I recall correctly, you said that you feel that you are somewhere between here and the Lord.

STORM: Sometimes I'm here and sometimes I'm there. I don't know how to explain that.

SWEENEY: Well, can you describe what it is like to be there with the Lord?

STORM: I guess the only way I've ever tried to describe it is by writing poems. It's been very unsatisfactory.

SWEENEY: Is there a poem, or two, that comes close to describing that experience?

STORM: I don't know if they do or not. Here is one:

    blessed
        Lord God

I sit alone in the sunset light
in the beauty of its golden haze
and cry out to You
blessed
    Lord God
You have given color to my eyes
and I cry out again
blessed
    Lord God
I will open the door of my heart
    to Your Glory
who have given color to my eyes
yet the door of my heart remains
closed
for who am I to open anything at all?

and so as dark night comes down
I sit alone in tears
waiting for Your Grace
to open the door of my heart
whenever it shall so please You
in Your glory
to enter there

thus waiting
suddenly I know . . .
You are already touching
    the very quick of my being
with wonder and love
for in Your Mercy
You have made no heart too small
to contain You

and behold the darkness
shines with Your Light

This is just as near as I can get to it.
SWEENEY: How do you deal with not being able to describe your
experience of God in poetry?

STORM: I guess I'm supposed to try, you know? I don't feel as if these are my poems, for one thing. Once I went into the confessional and told a priest that I was bothered by my terrible ego trip about being a poet. And he said, "I think if you would say a few 'Glory Be's,' it will help." Which I thought was pretty good.

Gradually, the poetry that somehow I write has become less and less *my* poetry. I think it is a gift from the Holy Spirit, that *I'm* supposed to write. And I don't worry at all anymore about whether it will get published or not. It will reach whomever it is supposed to reach.

SWEENEY: This experience of the Holy Spirit helping you when you're writing your poetry . . . Is there a particular kind of sensation?

STORM: I will sometimes just be lying on the couch, not feeling very good, just sort of floating, you know? And all of a sudden the words will come to me. And typically I don't forget them. A little later when I feel better I get up and write them down. It is a rather curious thing. I don't know why it should be that way. It didn't used to be that way when I wrote poetry. I'm not quite sure I write poetry. I know it's a prayer. I don't worry about whether it's poetry or not. I did really put myself through a lot of hard work learning the technique of writing particularly poetry, for quite a number of years.

SWEENEY: Today, August fifteenth, is your seventy-second birthday. How has your relationship with God changed over the years?

STORM: I was brought up what you might call a Unitarian. But nobody ever went to church.

I remember when I was very young I got hold of a Sunday School card that said, "God is love." A very nice little pink Sunday School card. And I remembered it for years, although I didn't know what it was talking about.

When I was ten my grandmother gave me a prayer book. Not a Bible. I was supposed to be doing my arithmetic homework one day, and I slipped up to the bookcase and found a red letter Bible. And I looked for the most possible red letters, and I found the Sermon on the Mount. And it moved me very, very deeply.

SWEENEY: At ten years old.

STORM: Yes. I just had never heard anything like it. I was deeply moved, almost to the point of shattering me. But my mother came in and caught me at it, and went down to the cellar, got a big stick and gave me a good beating because I was supposed to be doing my arithmetic.

From my early through my late teens, I had a sense of divine presence in nature. Very strong. I loved to go off in the woods, you know.

In my twenties, I got kind of sidetracked.

I remember the summer I was twenty-three, I had just graduated from college, and I was in Boston. And I saw what was a high Episcopal church—very beautiful and medieval looking. All carved wood. I used to stay after church reading in the pew, just very, very deeply moved by the sense of the place, you know. Not knowing a thing about what you were supposed to believe. And one of the monks came up to me and asked if I wanted to talk to him. And I became very confused and shy and said no and left. And in the course of the following year got very preoccupied with boyfriends, sex, and so forth.

I tried to earn a living as a writer, which was my skill at college—the English language. I tried it and found out that you had to be a liar and a hypocrite to earn your living as a writer. So I gave that up. Then I went back to music. I worked very hard at that. I was beginning to get somewhere with it. But this time I found out you also had to be a bit of a hypocrite at attracting pupils, which was much more important than being a good teacher. And that wasn't my idea of life.

So I didn't know what I was going to be or what I was going to do. And all of a sudden my financial backing for studying music was removed because of the Depression, and I was flat broke and had something close to a nervous breakdown. No one could do anything about the mess the world was in, I thought. I just didn't want to live. So I went around asking people what could be done about the mess the world was in. As a result, I became a Communist and remained one for twenty years. I was a reporter for *The Daily Worker* and things like that. But eventually I came to see that because the capitalists were wrong was no reason that the Communists were right.

SWEENEY: What was your experience of God at this time?

STORM: That was a strange thing. I was going into my fifties. I thought things through. I changed my mind about the mess the world was in. I decided to see what I could do for people. I thought love might be the answer. I started working with kids in a settlement house. This was up in Toronto, where I had escaped this Joseph McCarthy thing. And I kept bumping into significant things. For instance, I went to the beach and I found this stone. Hold it up and look at the light through it. It really isn't an emerald. It's a pebble that came from a piece of igneous rock. Apparently it came down from the Canadian Shield.

SWEENEY: It's beautiful.

STORM: It's the oldest rock in North America. Probably the oldest rock in the world. But anyway, this stone seemed to have something to tell me. Eventually, I decided that what it had to tell me was that God is in everything he made, in some sense. This is beauty from the center of the earth somehow coming out and being washed into a pebble. Isn't that amazing? There's an awful lot to it.

The next thing I heard of was Lao-Tse and the Apocalypse. They just came sticking their noses out at me in bookstores, saying, "You want me." So I started my mystic approach toward a spiritual level, an explanation of God's presence, with Oriental philosophy, and ended up a Catholic. Isn't that funny? You like my rock?

SWEENEY: Yes. A lot.

STORM: A couple of times people have tried to swipe it from me because it's so beautiful, but it always insisted on coming back. So I can't give that away.

Now, this is a funny way to explain the answer to your questions. Does it at all?

SWEENEY: Yes. I think every person has a story or history which is the vehicle through which he or she discovers God. And in addition to that history, there are, in some people's lives, specific moments such as this rock, when one becomes aware that God is present in all of creation. In these moments the whole of history is highlighted, summed up, capsulized. Those are the moments I'm trying to get at most. It's not because I value those moments more than all the history that leads up to them, but because in everybody's life there are millions of details; and if some people are able to pinpoint and articulate their precise transitions towards God or their understanding of God's activity in their lives, it makes it much easier for others who are not quite so articulate to say, "Ah, I understand," or "Yes, I see." And that's one of the reasons I'm interested in doing this book.

Who are you to God? It's the inverse of the first question, who is God to you? Who are you to God? How do you think God looks upon you?

STORM: I think God loves me. Sometimes I wonder why.

SWEENEY: How do you think he looks on you?

STORM: I really just couldn't . . .

SWEENEY: One of the reasons I ask that question is that when you love another person and you believe that other person loves you, a relationship forms. And in a relationship of love, obviously knowledge is acquired. And certainly in human relationships we begin to understand more and more about our*selves* through our understanding of the other person; how that other person regards us, how the other person speaks to us. Obviously, with a relationship with God we don't have that first hand feedback. And yet there are people who are terribly in love with God. I'm just wondering if your love, your knowledge, reaches into perhaps his knowledge of you.

STORM: There's nothing he doesn't know about me. He knows everything about me. The astonishing thing is that knowing everything about me, he accepts me. It's really quite astonishing. Does that help a little? Oh, I can't resist this. It's a poem.

> How can I ever get rid
> of my unedified id?

Here's another poem. Do you like this poem?

> In brief, dark ecstasies your crawling flesh
> is thunderous with beauty. You have led
> my feet strange paths, walking within a mesh
> of earth and sea and blood, passion spread.
>
> My waiting breasts are lovely with desire,

my whole slim body garnished for your taking.
My veins are petulant and run with fire
under your touch who gave my flesh its waking.

But lover, it was very strange last night
and terrible, too.
While you were sleeping the white
stars crowded over me and all their light was mine,
      without you.

Then you heard me weeping. I housed the wonder
      you would never know.
I cannot share my silence. Let me go.

I didn't know it was God I was writing about. What lover could
possibly be sufficient?
SWEENEY: I just have one final question. You've experienced a
lot. You've lived a long time. You've written poetry about God,
life, nature, and so on. I guess what I want to ask you is, is there
one thing, one statement, that sums up your deepest feelings?
STORM: Will you bear with me? I have two poems . . .

from this window at night
where the only sky I see
is man's violet neon glow
above the crowds of city lights
that pierce the dark with their lonely human cries

suddenly I remember the fiery agony of the stars
how they appear from a mountain slope
like shining peace

yet how unspeakably they must yearn
to explode into darkness

O the joyous endlessness of God
who is Maker
and the endless torment of God
who is Lover!

I am only a small candle
yet my flesh burns at times

with the fire of the Spirit
so that I seem to guess
something of both Maker and Lover
but I know nothing

* * *

silent Music
unshouting Trumpet
unsinging Flute
Stillness beyond knowing
dark Shining
most gracious visage of invisible Light
from You come all these:

water echo
      vision flow
toccata of laughter and sobs
        of pulse beats
            innumerable cries
polyphonic embroidery of flower
                    of child
                    of bird and wave and star

pallor out of glow
rainbow out of pallor
lark song in heart of rock
delicate and invulnerable bud of joy
        out of thorny stem
mysterious dialogue of sound and sight
sacrament of touch
from You come these

pattern on pattern
and pattern out of pattern
intangible caress of air
kiss of endless sky

KURT VONNEGUT, JR.

Palm Sunday, Deadeye Dick, Cat's Cradle, Slaugh-terhouse Five—these are but a few of the novels Kurt Vonnegut has written. I interviewed him in his Greenwich Village studio, where he introduced me to his daughter, Edith. She was working on her latest painting, but she stopped it to listen to her father's "experience" of God.

SWEENEY: Who or what is God to you?

VONNEGUT: Well, everybody (who grew up in a family situation) has their hereditary religion. I did, and for at least four generations my family has been proudly skeptical of organized religion. The first immigrant to this country named Vonnegut was a Catholic who became anti-clerical. And one recently came here because there wasn't going to be all this popery over here, particularly out in Indiana, where he settled. I was so devoted to that scheme in my bones that I would have been skeptical if I would have been raised a Catholic or any other religion.

This strain of religious skepticism is very strong in America. Mark Twain and H. L. Mencken, though from very different backgrounds, are examples of this. Both were extremely proud of behaving decently. They did this not from fear of hell or because of a promise of heaven but because behaving well was reason enough in itself. This they both did without organized religion. This is secular humanism, of course, which isn't thought much of in Texas.

So you ask me what God is to me? It would be pretty much the Unitarian God, where spring is celebrated and where there is a feeling of something terribly important going on in the universe, something unified, and awareness of that. My brother is a scientist and a religious skeptic like me. He tries to be aware of every moment—somebody having created quite a clock here, or whatever it is, and being deeply interested in how it works.

SWEENEY: Looking back over your life, have there been any major shifts in your awareness of God?

VONNEGUT: Well, there was one major shift with respect to organized religion. This was just before I went into battle in the second World War as I arrived at the front with a green division. We were facing the Siegfried Line, and I realized we were really going to do this thing and it seemed quite unremarkable to everybody. I wanted something said about it—some acknowledgment that something important was about to happen in our individual lives. And the Catholics set up a tent, but nobody else did. It was right behind the lines, so I went to religious services. I wanted some ritual acknowledgment that this was tremendously important to individuals. So, it's interesting that the man I went to the tent with remains my friend now. (He is a district attorney in Pennsylvania.) He told me to come to the tent with him if I wanted. I said yes, I'd better.

And then we were prisoners of war together. After the war he became a worse religious skeptic than any of my relatives. Broke his wife's heart by scorning Catholicism. I have no idea quite what caused him to do that.

SWEENEY: Did your being a prisoner of war have a negative effect on your faith or your understanding about it?

VONNEGUT: Well, it only confirmed what I had suspected in high school and even through my childhood—that God did not appear to be looking after us one by one. And from any statistical study I have been able to make, with my limited view, I was not "on the sparrow" nearly as I could tell, and I have seen many sparrows fall since then, and I've had my heart broken on that account. And so I judge God's performance, to the extent I can, and find him quite heartless. As a rationalist, I'd judge him the way I judge a president of the United States. This is a lousy president, this is a lousy God.

SWEENEY: Have there been moments in your life when you have felt the opposite—that God cared about you personally?

VONNEGUT: No. I have had the feeling that I was extremely lucky. I never felt that I was on any particular mission that he would be interested in—just winning at Las Vegas or something like that. That is my understanding of God. That he has based the whole thing on luck and this oft-quoted statement of Einstein's that you can't believe God is shooting dice with the universe. (I think it was a public relations statement and somehow took the curse off his weapons work and so forth. It was a cunning thing to say, and I would like to see the context of his statement, which I've never looked at.) My brother, for instance, an active scientist still, is dealing with atmospheric phenomena, the freezing of water and all that. And what he has had to confirm is that this actually is a crap shoot—the same thing does not happen again and again and again predictably. And of course, what astronomers are now confirming is this intolerable situation: they had hoped that God wasn't shooting dice with the universe and it appears he is.

SWEENEY: A little bit earlier you mentioned there was a kind of brilliance in creation. Is that your description of God, the one that orders that? I'm not quite clear on that point.

VONNEGUT: The way it is ordered is totally admirable—that animals are durable and work as well as they do. The pancreas, the liver, the thyroid. There is an extraordinary essay on the embryology of the eye which *Scientific American* published years ago. It is an example of one of the most superb pieces of writing in the history of science writing. This embryology could not have happened through any evolutionary scheme, as we now understand that process. Too much had to go on simultaneously, or we would be blind as bats. The wetting agents that keep the thing going renewing the rods and cones and all that so we can see. We can be a Thomas Edison or a Henry Ford and wonder how on earth they ever made this.

SWEENEY: What kind of image comes to your mind when you think of the term "God"?

VONNEGUT: Well, just because of the kind of animal I am, I'm gonna have to anthropomorphize almost anything, including other animals. And so, it is perfectly natural and human to imagine this as something manlike. And I've had no reason to fight against that because I don't write technical papers on it, and I'm in no sense a philosopher. So, I never had to oppose it. I'm perfectly willing to anthropomorphize it.

SWEENEY: For you, is God the one who orders nature?

VONNEGUT: He is the inventor, yes. And an extraordinary one because so many things work so well. It's so complicated. It wouldn't be that much trouble to manage if it were all gravel, if it were all dead, if the universe was a great big gravel pit. But the fact is that these animals and plants are so marvelously organized.

SWEENEY: So, God is the inventor or creator of what is. But in terms of your personal experience, God is not particularly involved or concerned about you? Is that correct?

VONNEGUT: Well, there would not be religious skeptics of my sort or like Mark Twain or Mencken if there weren't an enormous vanity operating there, and it is that God will think well enough of me when I get to heaven. You know—that I'll get right in anyway although I denied his existence. And this vanity is so enormous there is even the expectation that I'll be greeted as a colleague.

SWEENEY: That leads, then, to a more specific question. Who do you think you are to God?

VONNEGUT: I have not the slightest idea. Not an inkling. It's just total blank. I would give you some kind of answer, any kind of answer, but I have just no idea at all. I have a very strong sense of what other people think of me—but what he might think of me, God knows.

RICHMOND SHEPARD

I first met Richmond when he was playing the role of a mime in a television drama called "Clown of Freedom." This program was banned in several Latin American countries because its premise was that laughter and humor are not subject to the State. Richmond has been praised by some critics as America's foremost mime.

SHEPARD: Who is God to me? O.K. In a way there's a problem in the question because when you think in terms of who, you generally think in terms of a person, and I don't think of God as a personified being. Of course, I'm not a Christian, which may help to remove me one step from that. But having had spiritual experiences and contacts with a higher force as a result of being in the spiritual brotherhood of Subud, my idea or view of who or what God is changed radically away from classical teaching. It's not what I used to think it was. It's neither the old man with the beard, nor is it male or female. My experience with higher forces leads me to feel that God is the classic definition of omnipotent, omnipresent, and omniscient. So, if I say he, I'm not thinking in terms of a personified deity. I'm talking in terms of God being a high spiritual force that is the creator of the universe. He is everywhere, was before all things, and will be here after all things. This is the highest creative force for good, the creativity for growth, for evolution of the body and the spirit. In a way, my definition becomes almost a classical definition without the personification.

SWEENEY: How does that force relate to you? Or how do you relate to that force?

SHEPARD: Well, you'll have to take with a grain of salt anything I tell you about my personal experiences because they are experiences, and they don't compare with any particular teaching. Teachings you can argue with. If somebody says they have had an experience, you can say, well, maybe he has, or maybe he hasn't. The kind of experiences I'm talking about are the phenomena known as "receiving," which are referred to by St. Teresa, St. John of the Cross, and other mystics who experienced this process of being able to connect with "upstairs," being able to receive influence, guidance, information, etc., from contact with a higher spiritual force. This high spiritual force comes from God.

SWEENEY: How does the high spiritual force contact you? Or relate to you?

SHEPARD: How . . . I contact it by doing an exercise which we call latihan in the spiritual brotherhood called Subud. This exercise, which we do twice a week for half an hour, is a spontaneous contact with the power of God. And this power, this high spiritual force, has influenced my life more and more, and has given me guidance. It's opened certain doors for me, and it's closed others that used to be open. And the more I surrender to it and allow it to affect me, the more influence it has on my life. You always have a choice. You can receive that something's right for you, and then you have the choice whether to follow that path or not. Sometimes I don't follow that path.

SWEENEY: Can you give a specific example of one major decision that you were influenced by in terms of this "high spiritual force"?

SHEPARD: Sure. I was wondering whether or not to move to California. So I asked. Call it testing. I tested. I asked how would it be for me if I remained in New York, and I received this "feeling"; then I asked how would it be for me if I moved with my family to California, and I received a better manifestation, so I moved to California. It was a major event in my life. And that was a question of specifically asking what would be better for my life and my well being and my spiritual progress. Other times guidance will come spontaneously.

SWEENEY: So, you discern the effects within yourself even though the openness and intention is to receive the wisdom from another force, or from this higher force?

SHEPARD: From the higher force which is already in you and in everybody to some degree, and that people generally are not in contact with. With most people, their imagination and their mind are guiding their life. Now your mind, depending on the power of it, can be a tremendous tool, but if it's not going in the right direction of your soul, your spiritual being, then sometimes your mind can make the wrong decision. And all your talent, your imagination, and your intelligence are not working on your behalf. If you can receive guidance from a higher force, your mind becomes a tool of your soul and will then be working on your behalf. And all this talent, imagination, and power will be working for you. That's the difference. In a way, you might even say that you leave the responsibility in your life's path to God instead of to your mind. So, of course, if you receive something and don't follow it, you're on your own. If you receive it and do follow it, you're protected in a way.

SWEENEY: What do you think is the most important or vital way that this spiritual force relates to you in your life?

SHEPARD: Well, it's changed my relationship with the material world. I would say the material forces really had me by the grapes, as we put it, at one time and really moved me around. And year by year the material forces have relaxed their hold on me. I'm less affected by the power of physical objects, wealth, the accoutrements, the things that we wear around who we really are. It's also changed my relationship with life and death because I've had several experiences that have shown me that we, as an entity, can survive without our physical body.

Well, that's what happens when you die. You leave your physical body. And there's a kind of consciousness you can have if your spiritual body has been awakened, if your soul is alive. We feel since we can't take our eyes with us when we die, the material body dies. Well, you can't take your eyes and ears, but you can take the power of sight and the power of hearing if your spiritual body has grown and is awakened. Similarly, you can take the consciousness you feel. I don't know what the next chapter is. I don't know. I don't really know what it is to survive, to live, or whatever our life is after we leave the material body that lives on the material planet. But I've had enough evidence to show me from experience that there is something else. Now, that's a big surprise. You know, people hope there'll be something, they wonder if there'll be something, they're taught there's something, and yet, many of them don't believe it. So, to actually experience that there is something, that there is a possibility of survival after the physical body dies is quite interesting and startling, and it changes your relationship with living and dying. When my mother died I didn't want her to die. I felt in a way my children were cheated out of their grandmother and I felt really sad. But my relationship to her dying was different from the rest of my family. And the day after she died I had a very strong experience with her which had to do with her going on into the next world—an experience that was very far out and quite moving—the kind of experience that people don't generally have.

SWEENEY: What was the content of that experience?

SHEPARD: The content of the experience was during the latihan at Subud. She came to me, her spiritual body entered into me, and after a short time was propelled outward off of this planet. I don't know . . .

SWEENEY: And the feeling of her entering you, was what kind of feeling, what kind of emotion?

SHEPARD: It's hard to explain the feeling, it's hard to . . .

SWEENEY: But it wasn't disturbing, it wasn't upsetting?

SHEPARD: Oh no, it was just great, it just felt great! It was enveloping, it was absorbing in the contact and a way of giving her a feeling of security, and ssshh . . . shooting off fast and far. With the force, the spiritual force shooting her off so that the next day at the funeral she wasn't present. Sometimes you come to a funeral and you can sense that the person is still hanging around. They like to hang around the body for a few days. But she wasn't there. She wasn't present, only her body was present at the funeral. It was very interesting, the whole thing. It was an extraordinary experience.

I guess it would be hard for me to describe what it feels like to do latihan at Subud when we are in contact with the high spiritual force. You feel a kind of vibration in your body, and it may make you move a little, or it may make you make a sound, or it may make you feel something, or experience something, but as long as you are in a state of surrender, allowing it to work, it'll work. If you start concentrating or focusing, or thinking a lot, it'll fade out. But if you just let it do whatever it does, think whatever thoughts or do whatever happens, it will work on you. At the end of the half hour, you're in a changed state. Almost a little high from it.

SWEENEY: So the two effects of getting in contact with the spiritual force have been your understanding of life and death and your relationship to the material world. Were there any other major effects?

SHEPARD: Well, with those two things it affects everything you do. Your relationship with people. I experienced it stronger in the beginning than I do now. A great kinship with all other people. You begin to realize that you're all really part of the same thing and that your prejudices and actions that hurt other people are, in a way, hurting part of yourself. Now, this doesn't mean that I can always carry that out. This doesn't mean that I'm living a saintly life, by any means.

But at least part of me understands what right behavior is, or should be. I can say that in my work as a result of this contact I'm helped and guided in the right direction and my work goes more easily.

SWEENEY: Is there any other major way you have in relating to this high spiritual force other than being passive and perceptive?

SHEPARD: Not specifically. In a way, it's an act of surrender. Now, a short time after I began to approach the Subud, I had some experiences and I became interested in all mystical literature. I read the Old Testament, the New Testament, the Hindu mystics, the Chinese mystics, and, as I mentioned, I read St. Teresa, St. John of the Cross, and the Koran. And I began to be interested in what other people had received, were receiving, and their methods. I went to monasteries. I went to the Trappist Monastery in Massachusetts, St. Joseph's Abbey, to see what they were into. I went to all their Masses from 3:30 in the morning on to get a feeling and to talk to these people. Trappists don't talk, but they will assign someone who can talk to you about their methods or ways of trying to climb the spiritual mountain, or trying to connect with God, or upstairs, or whatever you want to call it. But to be able to receive. And . . . what I understood they are doing is starving the material forces to death by the austere life they live—sleeping on a piece of wood with some straw, eating bread and coffee for breakfast, praying and not talking, and working hard physically, with no temptations. There are no outside material forces, nothing to excite the passions, nothing to covet. They are gradually quieting the material forces and the passions, and you can see in the eyes of some of these men, the brothers, some veils have been lifted. It really felt nice. I felt that there were some other men there who didn't feel as nice. They were displaying what you might call spiritual pride. "Look at me, I'm so holy, look what I'm doing." So that in a way is worse.

But then I went to the monastery out here, the desert of Valyermo, where these really nice Benedictines are trying; they're not trying to climb the spiritual mountain; they're not trying to starve the passions and the material forces to death. They are trying to lead a Christian life of warmth and love and brotherhood. But they're not trying to make this, what you might call spiritual progress of "being" development. This is the development of the Being mentioned by Aldous Huxley in his last book, *Island,* where he was on a very confused spiritual search at the end of his life, where he tried everything. He said, right doing and right being are two different things. Right doing does not provide, provoke, develop right being. He said right being will automatically provide right doing. But right doing will only make you a pillar of society.

SWEENEY: Well, that's not bad.

SHEPARD: Which isn't bad. So these Benedictines are attempting right doing without the struggle, or whatever it is—the real attempt to reach upstairs. So they have an air-conditioned chapel, and they sleep on a mattress, and they eat meat three times a week. It's not an austere life. It's trying to be good and kind. It's terrific. It really felt nice there.

SWEENEY: Well, in light of all your reading and visiting different places in your own spiritual journey, what is your conclusion regarding these various ways to God?

SHEPARD: I think the first step is take a step toward reaching God. And anybody who thinks his way is the only way hasn't found the way. There are many paths up the mountain. I'm in favor of, and think it's good for people to take, whatever path they want. Whether it be through meditation or through their religion or whatever, at least they're trying to reach upstairs. They're making some attempt, in a way, whether they find it or not, to receive what's right for them, or what is God's will for them.

I think there's only one prayer—some of my friends disagree with me—the only prayer is to be able to receive God's will for me. And maybe the second step would be to have the strength to carry it out. People pray for a car, for more money, to get that girl, or whatever, but it may not be right for their spiritual development to have those things at that time. Of course, my will doesn't always know; it should be Thy will.

SWEENEY: How do you distinguish between the will of God and . . .

SHEPARD: . . . the will of your passions and material forces?

SWEENEY: Right.

SHEPARD: In time I've come to be able to differentiate the sources of my impulses. People who are on Subud for a while eventually begin to do this process called "testing," where you ask the question and do latihan. The answers received don't test alone. We have a group of men who have been doing it for some time, who will answer test questions for the members; then after a year or two maybe the member will test with the helpers, and then later they will test by themselves. You can begin to sense when your channel becomes more and more clear.

SWEENEY: So you're introduced into this discernment through a group of people first. And then later on, once you have that strength through the group, you can do it alone?

SHEPARD: Yeah. There's very little written about Subud. We do no proselytizing, and there are centers all over the world. There's even a Catholic monastery in France where some of the brothers have been doing it for fifteen years.

SWEENEY: Is there a book or something?

SHEPARD: No, not really. Incidentally, the reason anyone can experience latihan in Subud is that nothing is taught. Absolutely nothing is taught, so that people in various religions, or no religion at all, can do it.

For a year and a half when I was in Oakland, I didn't talk to anybody at the center. I figured the people there were a bunch of religious nuts who didn't know what they were talking about; I went in anyway, I did the latihan for half an hour, and I split without saying a word to anybody. Nobody told me what to do, how to do it. By the time a year and a half went by, I had enough experience to realize something was going on. Then I talked to people. By the time two years went by, my whole theology had gone from being an atheist, a complete doubter, because I'd never received any evidence that there was anything higher spiritually, to one who realized that something was going on, that there is another world, a spiritual world, and a soul is beginning to develop. That's a profound change in two years. Now I've been doing it for fifteen years.

SWEENEY: So latihan refers to the experience which puts you in contact?

SHEPARD: Yes. It's the formal exercise we do twice a week for half an hour. The force, in a way, is with you all the time after a while. It's a constant little vibrational hum inside of you. And I've had the experience of driving along a winding mountain road and suddenly felt the latihan very strongly. I allowed it to work and felt it turn the wheel and pull the car over; and just then a car came careening around the corner that would have hit me if I hadn't pulled out of the way. I felt quite protected at that moment. Your intuitive faculties are enhanced. You can understand and tune into other people's state, but this is kind of a bonus. You also tend to be physically healthy. Apparently the soul likes to live in a healthy body, and the force begins to work in every cell in your body.

In a way, everything I'm saying is very sectarian because I'm talking about an esoteric spiritual brotherhood and experience, and I'm using terminology that's really not common experience.

SWEENEY: Were you baptized, or raised . . .

SHEPARD: I'm Jewish. I was raised Jewish, but my family was never religious. In fact, I went to a Methodist school in Georgia for several years—Emory University—and went to church a lot when I was there. I was always interested in what was going on. I went to Baptist churches, Presbyterian churches. I had friends who were Catholic. I went to Catholic churches. I was looking to see what people were into and if I felt any contact. I never was attracted to organized religion at all. My interests changed when I began to have spiritual experiences, and when I read all the literature I realized there was something behind it. And the fact that religions may be administered by lesser men than the founders of the religion doesn't mean that there isn't a spiritual truth behind the whole thing. Unfortunately, many clergymen do not understand the sources of the things they're talking about. So today my children go to religious school at our temple. In a way, to get a cultural background more than a religious. I still do not find great content, great spiritual content, in churches or synagogues. I find in a religion something that's good for the heart. In other words, it makes people feel good. They feel an emotional content, but feeling good in the heart and the emotional content are different from real contact with the highest source. So people do the best they can. They follow teachings. They try to do good. They try to do right, but if your soul is wrong, it's very hard to carry out what your mind tells you to do.

SWEENEY: In your lifetime, especially in the past fifteen years, would there be one experience of this spiritual force that has moved you most profoundly?

SHEPARD: There have been a couple. One was the incident with my mother the day after she died, others were "experience dreams," dreams that start in an unconscious state but are so vivid and so real that they seem like reality, even after you wake up. But these are the big, far-out ones. The real change has been. . . . My mother was a psychiatric social worker, and after I had been in Subud a number of years—she was living in California and I was living in New York—she came to New York. Now, psychiatrists tend not to believe in anything mystical. They have a different orientation. They don't believe in that whole other world. They deal with man's life here and now. She said to me after I was in Subud maybe four or five years, "I don't believe in anything mystical, but whatever Subud is, I like it because of what it's done to you." I said, what did it do? I can't see what's happened. I hadn't seen her in three years. She said, "You're no longer angry." I had been a very angry, very hostile person. In 1960, the night before my show opened in New York, I jumped over the table in a restaurant and punched my producer.

I had studied karate for a year, as there was fighting on the street. If some guy on the street corner said "hey, the god-damned Jews," I had to go over and punch him. I still have some of that anger and hostility in me now, but compared to what it was. . . . Well, I was a raving maniac at times. She said, "You're not angry all the time." The anger had, in a way, flown out and been dissipated.

What I mentioned before, the relationship with the material world—I feel now that if wealth was to come, I don't think it would have me. I know it wouldn't have me like it would have had me, like it has many of the people in Hollywood who are moved by the power of material objects. The Cadillac says buy me, and they buy it. They can't afford it. So over a long period of time those are the real profundities: the lack of anger, the freedom from material dominance.

SWEENEY: Is there a consciousness associated with this spiritual force?

SHEPARD: Well, I don't know. I can tell you that we've tested this out a few times. If you're in Subud and you have a question that you would like tested, you can send the same question to the group in England, in Indonesia, in Paris, in London, or in New York, and without them knowing you, they'll all get the same answer because the answer comes from that same source which is everywhere. I've seen that happen again and again. So it shows that it's everywhere. The fact that the answers tend to be correct implies to me that it really knows a lot. That it is omniscient in some way.

SWEENEY: The reason I ask that is I'm wondering if you have any idea how this consciousness or this omniscience regards you?

SHEPARD: I don't think that you can say I'm in contact with God—he's busy—but maybe with the power of God, or the force from, or the relationship with God. I have the feeling that this power wants each of us to fulfill our own personal destiny to the best, the most efficiently, and in the best way. And I feel we receive help when we surrender to the power of God. We allow God to work in us, and we allow the highest spiritual forces to guide us and to lead us. We are protected and taken care of, so that there is some kind of interest. I know Billy Graham has written a book about angels. I glanced through it and I wasn't sure what he's really driving at, but I think there are, in a way, angels. Not in the classic religious sense of a little winged being, but of aides and helpers that can help us. When the lining came off my tire on the freeway one day, I know those angels were flapping their wings real hard to keep me from getting killed.

SWEENEY: Do you love that high spiritual force, that omniscience?

SHEPARD: That's interesting because that's a big word in Christianity.

SWEENEY: Yes, it is. In Judaism, too.

SHEPARD: More in Christianity. That's interesting, do I love that force? Yeah. I love having the contact. I love having the security of it, and there's a feeling of reverence and respect. I understand that in Russian there are something like twelve different words for love: love for your father, love for your brother, love for a friend, love for a cousin, love for God. In English, we have one word.

SWEENEY: Well, even more precisely: Do you love the source of that power, and that force?

SHEPARD: I feel like a son—I do feel filial love, but it's more than that. It's worship, respect, confidence in, reliance on, trust, all those things that are going to take care of me. So, yeah, it's very strong. The word love is bandied about too much.

SWEENEY: Yes, I know.

SHEPARD:. . . but it includes all that whole list I just said. And, in a way, most of all love is trust and confidence in another, which is the strongest kind of love. It's not a cowering, fearful love. I'm not afraid of it. I feel more like a son, and you shouldn't really be afraid of your father. Your father can be stern, but he protects you. He takes care of you. That's more of the feeling it is. In fact, if he's the King, I feel like a prince.

SWEENEY: You're very fortunate.

SHEPARD: It's much bigger than the English concept of love, bigger and stronger and more powerful. It's not physical. It's a different kind of hug you get from God.

VICTOR AFFONSO

Born and now living in India, Victor Affonso is a dynamic, charismatic Jesuit priest. For several years he lived in Los Angeles while doing degree work at the University of California. During this time he was forced to confront his skepticism toward "born again Christians," healings, and Kathryn Kuhlman.

AFFONSO: I was brought up in a typically Catholic background in India. We said the rosary and other prayers every day. We went to Mass every Sunday without question. So for me, God was a person who was responsible for my being, gave us everything that we asked, and who took care of our family. As long as I didn't have a bad experience, God was up in his heaven and I was down on earth. It was a good experience, a community experience, but nothing more than that.

I would give my life for this God; but then, when I was sixteen, my mother died. It was a terrible shock to me because my mother was very religious. I literally gave up on God. She almost died giving birth to her last child, but the doctor saved both their lives. Two months after the child was born she went to the hospital, and died of heart failure by being given the wrong injection, or something like that. Then I said, if there is a God in heaven—you know this famous problem of evil towards the innocent—I said there is no Jesus in God because he didn't take care of her.

But now I can see my experience of the Blessed Virgin Mary, that Mary had played an important part in my life because of my mother. Then I began to pray only to her, not trusting anymore in Jesus. Jesus and God were far in the background, but I knew there was a Divine Being out there and Mary was one of the powerful intercessors who gets things for us. And then, after she had

101

answered many of my prayers, I came once again to trust in this so-called Divine Power, whose representation for me was Mary. And finally, going through an experience with the Jesuits with whom I was studying, and through the spiritual exercises, I knew there was Jesus. It was Mary who said if you really love me now and you trust me, I can answer your prayers, but it is Jesus who really answers your prayers. So, between this devotion to Mary and the Jesuit schooling that I had, I knew Jesus as the one who could solve all the problems throughout the world.

At the age of twenty-three I wanted to escape the terrible problem of poverty in India, with beggars living and dying in the streets. I had everything I wanted, so I didn't have to bother about this poverty in the country. But it came to me very strongly that these people could be helped. I felt there must be a solution to this, and I could see there was no human solution. Then there must be a God who has a solution for this.

In 1956 I became a Jesuit. I wanted Jesus to use me and my talents to help the poor, even though I didn't know how this would happen. So then I went through the whole Jesuit experience. And yet, I don't feel that I experienced Jesus. I meditated on him through the prayers, and all that. I couldn't go through those compulsory prayers in the Society of Jesus. I didn't like compulsory breviaries. I didn't like read-out prayers in church, but I went through them, and they helped me. The Imitation of Christ, and all that. But I knew that I was giving my life for a Jesus whom I did not experience. He was out there, I believed, because I was taught it by my superiors. I believed it because my prayers were answered sometimes. I knew the only solution that might make my life useful in this world would be to try this God out; but I had not experienced him even right up to ordination. And I liked what comes in ordination—people respect and honor you because you're a priest, and you feel that you've been given a special privilege in preaching the Word in the Kingdom of God. And yet, I preached like any lecturer who studies the Scriptures and gives it out to people. I did not know the difference; I thought I was, you know, a religious person.

In the early seventies I moved to Los Angeles, to study communications at UCLA. I wanted to bring this knowledge back to India to help educate the poor.

On Pentecost Sunday in 1972, I had prepared a sermon on the Holy Spirit to give the parishioners in Brentwood, who are very rich. Here I had come to the richest parish in the world, and I saw how stingy they were about giving to the poor. They didn't understand the question of poverty. They waste food. I was angry within myself, and my anger came out in the sermons. I was getting emotionally involved with this whole thing. I had given my life for this, and I could see Christians who had the money and could help. They were coming to Sunday Mass; they were saying they were good Catholics; and they couldn't even feel for their brothers. And I really got angry, the message kept coming to me from the Lord: "Do not be angry with my people because they have not experienced poverty like you." I had asked them to travel to India and experience it; but they said no, they cannot stand the poverty, and what they saw on television. They tried to erase it from their minds.

So here it was, Pentecost Sunday, and I was going to tell the people about the Holy Spirit and how it changes hearts, and how you have to give yourself to the Lord. And do you know, that very morning I got this terrible pain in my back, and I could not give this sermon. I was taken to the hospital, paralyzed from my head to my waist. And as I was being rushed to the hospital in an ambulance, I asked the Lord, why? Why, today, when I wanted to speak on the Holy Spirit?

When I was in the hospital, a Sister came in and told me some Charismatics wanted to pray over me. I said, "Nothing doing, not Charismatics, I don't want them." Because I had had this terrible experience at Loyola University, and it really turned me off. (You see, I'm the typical Jesuit who has studied all the adversaries against Pentecostalism, against emotionalism, against all this nonsense.) At Loyola, during Mass, the people began to speak during the sermon. I didn't like that—only the priest can preach. And during the kiss of peace, everybody embraced one another, women and all and I thought, here goes my vow of chastity. Now, see, I joined at the age of twenty-three, and I know what it is to be with women—and I'm one of the more openminded in the Society— but something was telling me that this was going off the track of my normal priesthood. Then, after Communion these people

start humming like bees, making this funny sound, each in his . . .
I'd never heard of Tongues before, so I felt that these people and
the Jesuits were going off their rocker right there in a Jesuit
University. I wondered if Father General knew about it. These
were the thoughts that went though my mind.

Okay. So I was lying in the hospital, and these so-called Charismatics were going to come and pray for me. Before I could
protest, in they came with big disarming smiles on their faces, and
said, "Father, we're going to pray for you!" I said, "Nothing doing!
You're not going to pray for me, and please don't put your hands
on me." So they said, "Oh, no, this is a daily prayer." And I said,
"Nothing doing, only the bishop has put his hand on my head.
And you are not going to put your hand on my head. So you can
pray for me from far away, okay?" They said, "No Father." They
came and they literally pushed—I wouldn't advise any Charismatic to do this; it would be a traumatic experience for somebody else—but God gave me the grace maybe to pray at that time.
So when they put their hands on my head, I said, "Lord, Father in
Heaven, please forgive them for they know not what they do."
This was my prayer, and especially if there was a Protestant
among them; I was dead against Protestants. (In '72, mind you, in
India we had much more strong feelings against Protestants,
because we never knew who they were.) And here I was, flat on
my back, and as soon as they prayed over me, a shock passed
through my body. I said, "I don't know what spirit this is." And
they left with smiles on their faces, and a pile of books in their
wake on the bed. The book on the top was Kathryn Kuhlman's *I
Believe in Miracles.* But I said, "No, not this person." I didn't know
what kind of a challenge this was. And Kathryn Kuhlman of all
people! I really didn't like her because I felt she could destroy
Christian faith with all her theatrics.

I began to ask the Lord, "Lord, why this sudden change that
came over me after they prayed? Why did you do this to me
today?" And this thought came to me: "You wanted to preach to
my people, but I think I can teach you a lot more. Go and pray
with my people, pray with them, visit them, suffer with them.
You're not going to preach too much. You're going to speak to
them my Word, the Gospel, not your prepared sermons. And I

will teach you how to speak to my people, because when they come to church, I have already spoken to them, and I have called them to church. They have come to be fed with the Word, and what you are going to say is going to confirm them on that day."

And I thought, the Lord wants me to pray more, maybe. He wants me to reunderstand what it is to preach to people about the Holy Spirit. So I left it at that. I didn't know what he was teaching me.

Okay. That night I put the TV on. Now this is what I call walking in the Spirit. I began to watch everything that happened to me then, to see what the Lord was doing to me. I never did that before, even though I was a Jesuit. I had had a good experience of people filling all my desires and wishes as soon as I gave over my world to him. That experience I always had as a Jesuit. Whenever I said, "Okay, Lord, take me fully," then he gave me a hundredfold. He fulfilled me with many blessings, so in that way I was always happy with the Lord, but now I was going into a new experience with God. And that night when I put on the TV who comes on but Kathryn Kuhlman! I said, "No!" Then I flicked the automatic switch and it came back to the same channel; it was fixed on that channel—Kathryn Kuhlman. I said, "Well, for heaven's sake, Lord, why are you trying to fool me with this?" So I turned off the set, and the next day, I called the repairman and asked him to fix it.

And he did. Then I put on the set, and on came a Spanish man and his wife, and they were speaking about how she had been paralyzed for thirteen years and then was healed all of a sudden by prayer. And I thought, I believe these people because they are Catholics. Now, see, I was prejudiced. I thought maybe they had gone to Lourdes, or something like that, and must have got a miracle. Then the camera turned, and next to this woman is Kathryn Kuhlman. It was her show. But do you know something? Something happened already, the Lord was really giving me a grace. He opened me for the first time to listen to Kathryn Kuhlman. I would never have listened to her. And I began to listen to her, and she was saying, "You know that I'm nobody; in fact, I shouldn't be a minister here, I'm a woman. I shouldn't be here, but the Lord appoints me, and he can appoint any human being. I don't preach, I don't heal, I only take the Word of God and give it to the people, and when I'm speaking the Word of God, people get healed. And I give the word of knowledge." And she said, "Give all the glory to God, I'm nobody." For the first time I listened, and I said, "This is a good woman." I stopped looking at her long sleeves and the backdrop of the television and everything else, and I listened to her. As soon as that show was over, I took out the book, *I Believe in Miracles,* and began to read it. My mind opened to Kathryn Kuhlman, Protestant, and to healings.

I was one month in that hospital, and I walked out of there without an operation. I began to learn how to pray with Charismatics. I learned of the prayer group at St. Martin's, of Sister Ignatius, and I went there to pray; little by little I was entering into a new field. Suddenly I began to open the Scripture, and something happened to me. For the first time, Terry, I could read between the lines, and every word of Scripture jumped out at me. The Old Testament began to tell me things that I never heard before, giving me a new life for the people. Whenever I had a need, for anything, I went to the Scripture, opened it, and it spoke to me. You know, it's something like the experience of young people who have fallen in love. When they find the one they love, what happens? They leave their father, their mother, they can be called fools, they will leave their money, they will leave their palace, and they will run to the one they love. That is exactly the experience I went through in '72 after this. Not when I joined the Society of Jesus. Yes, I followed him, it was an intellectual experience, I tell you, conceptual and everything else. I believe there was faith there, but it was not an experiential faith like I have now. It is richer, very much richer, and now I know what the experience was of the first Christians.

This was a Pentecostal experience. This is what I think I went through soon after these people prayed for me. I was on fire, the word of the Lord came on completely strong. So when I went to say Mass, the whole Mass to me was so much different. I read the Scriptures, but I wasn't preparing sermons anymore. When I faced the people, suddenly I was speaking the Scripture and teaching them the Scripture and referring to Scripture, and it was flowing out like I had prepared all my life. It was a different experience.

Suddenly people were responding to me in a way I had never felt before. Before they had said, "Father, good sermon, fantastic sermon, I like the story." But they didn't change their lives. Now they were coming and telling me, "Father, I saw Jesus, I experienced Jesus," and there were tears in their eyes. I had never seen this, even after many years as a Jesuit.

Not long after I left the hospital, a Jesuit friend of mine from India arrived in Los Angeles to study at UCLA. Jim had health problems, complained a lot. I asked some doctor friends of mine to examine him. They discovered that he had terminal cancer of the bone, and they gave him only two months to live.

I asked myself, what can I do? I'm about to finish my thesis, and I'm leaving for India in July. My friend is going to die. I better take him home to die. And the housekeeper came and said, "Father, take him to Kathryn Kuhlman." And I said, "Okay, I'll do this last thing. I'll see if Jim will agree to this. If he believes in miracles, let's go and try it." And we went there; and there were about seven hundred people outside the auditorium, and about seven to eight thousand people inside. And, believe it or not, a man came right up to me and said, "Father, would you like to get inside?" Now, there were hundreds of other priests and nuns who couldn't get inside, and he came first to me.

I said, "Sure, but I didn't come by myself. My brother here is sick." So the man brought us in. And, do you know, we landed right on the stage, in the front row, where Kathryn Kuhlman was going to speak? So I sat and began reading the Bible, and Jim couldn't even sit up, you know, his bones were aching.

Anyway, a man called me in the wings, and said, "Father, I'm very interested in knowing what you two Indian priests are doing over here." And I said, "Well, I'm a television student at UCLA; I'm going back to India to educate the 60-80% illiterate people." And I told him the story about Jim. He said, "Okay." So I started back to my seat. A lady came and said, "Hello, Father, I'm so happy that you've come here." I said, "Well, I also am but, you know, it's my brother who's got cancer that I'm worried about." And I looked into her eyes and saw it was Kathryn Kuhlman. She held my hand, and I said, "Kathryn, I recognize you now, I see your eyes, but I tell you, I never would have come here because I've never liked your shows." And she gave a big laugh, and I said, "No, as a television student, I feel that you are really destroying Christian television, and I would never have come here if not for my brother there who is dying of cancer. I wish you could pray for him."

She answered, "Oh, I'm so happy you've come. What is your work?" I told her about my media work and all that. Then I went back to my place. The service started and she came in. The singing and prayer were beautiful. I tell you I had never experienced all this prayer and community in the Catholic church. I've really experienced the presence of the Lord. Above all, I think it was because there was a mixture of all denominations. And there was the experience of Jesus. I can't explain this.

When the prayer was over, she said to the people, "I've something to tell you, something very important to tell you." She never does this normally, right at the start of the service. "There is a man from India I want you to meet." I said, "Jim, get ready because she is going to pray for you." She went on, "And I would like you to meet Father Victor Affonso." I said, "No, I'm not coming to speak to anybody. I am not going to speak to this Protestant congregation on the Kathryn Kuhlman show." But the people said, "Father, she is calling you." And immediately the spot came up on me. I said, "No, it is for him, this is the man who needs to be healed." "No," they said, "go forward."

So, I went. She said, "Father, would you mind speaking to the people?" I said, "No, I'm not prepared to speak. What am I going to tell them, Kathryn, that I don't like your shows?" "Yes," she said, "go and tell them that you don't like my show."

And I did something then that people said afterward that nobody else had done. I went forward and kissed her. Men used to keep away from her like she had an aura about her. She never wanted it to be that way, but they always stayed away from her. I, a Catholic priest, went and kissed her and people loved that idea.

I told them I didn't like this show, and the people had a good laugh. And she had a good laugh—this convinced me of her humility—you know, a true person of God. And then suddenly Scripture came to me in a way that had never happened to me before, and out came this whole thing that the Lord has put very strongly in my heart. "All authority is given to me," I said. "Go ye, therefore, to all nations, teaching them all that I have taught you and baptizing them in the name of the Father, and of the Son and of the Holy Spirit. And behold I am with you until the end of time." I said, "India is waiting, the whole world is waiting. We are being fed and overfed with Scripture and you have a duty to go out and preach the Word, and we priests, above all."

And do you know, that during that day I saw hundreds of healings and I was fully convinced. At first, I was skeptical; I figured this was a put-on show; but I saw a young boy weeping who could never have walked—if you paid him a million dollars, he couldn't—he was running up and down the stage and crying, "Jesus, Jesus!" His parents had given up on him because he could never walk in his life, and there he was almost . . . I could see the life coming into his limbs. I saw several miracles there that were genuine as far as I was concerned. You just couldn't tell me to prove that again even if there were no doctors. Anyway, I saw before my eyes miracles for the first time. Kathryn began praying over me and was trying to "slay" me in the Spirit. I never knew what a slaying in the Spirit was. I objected. I didn't want to be slain in the Spirit, and she prayed over me that I would be a great apostle for the Lord on television and everything else, but I didn't want to be slain in the Spirit. I went and sat down in my seat after I had finished the whole thing. At the end of the show I said, "Lord, why did you bring me here? She's not even praying for Jim. He's not even healed!" Then, I saw him crossing his legs—Jim couldn't do that before. And I said, "Jim, you're crossing. . . ." And he said, "No, no, I've still got pain." Kathryn came straight towards him, spoke to me, and said, "Take this little Indian priest back to India healed." With that, Jim jumped up like an electric shock and fell flat on the ground.

SWEENEY: Say that again, I missed that . . .

AFFONSO: She walked right up to Jim, but spoke to me, pointing to him and said, "Take this little Indian priest back to India healed."

SWEENEY: Healed?

AFFONSO: Healed . . . healed of cancer. And Jim jumped up and fell flat to the ground. The fellow couldn't walk, just fell flat! And out . . . conked out. "By God," I said, "she's going to ruin this guy."

But I had seen during the service that many of these people who were walking for the first time in their lives had been thrown by Kathryn to the ground. And I said, "Maybe this is the work of God." So, I raised Jim up again and I made him stand just like a plank, hanging almost like dead, in perfect peace. And I said, "Jim, how are you?" And he said, "Okay." Then a person behind me said, "Father, there's no need to hold him." And I let him go, and Jim went wham, again, to the ground. And I went right over him, on the ground. I must tell you, Terry, it was not falling on the ground. I have fallen many times in my life—in hockey, football, in every way. But this was like somebody held me in their power, and just took me, and made me sleep, or made me lie down. It was as if some power just took me down. And I was lying on Jim! And I heard the people clap. I don't know why, maybe because they saw me do this thing at the beginning. But I was concerned about Jim, then, and I forgot about myself, and the Lord's power just put me down.

When I got up, I saw people falling like waves as Kathryn passed through. They were just falling, nuns and priests, everybody, just collapsing, and they were happy! This was my first experience of this, of God working among men today through healings and other signs. When I got out, many people came to me and said, "You know, Father, it was not the miracles that impressed us, it was what you said. You spoke about India and the millions of people who wanted to come to Jesus, and that the Gospel has to be preached, and those words really touched our hearts, and all the time we were praying for India." Then I knew how the Holy Spirit works. I had not prepared that speech.

Jim went back to the hospital, and you know what? He walked out of it. The nuns said, "Father, he's in great trouble, this man has to take the cobalt treatments." And Jim believed the doctors more than me. He was almost walking again, but he had some sickness left in him, and in his heart of hearts would not believe in the healing. I don't know why. He wouldn't go back to India with me but instead continued the cancer treatment. I can't explain it. If people are not healed literally I have no answer, believe me.

Now, I had never healed anybody. But this was another experience the Lord would give me. You ask who is my God? I was about to experience him, his power. And then only would that word from Scripture come to life in me again: "You go where you are sent, and in my name, you will cast out demons. You will heal the sick. . . . You are going into this world to show that I have given you my power, and greater things than these you are going to do. If you're going to stand in my name, you're not going to be anxious about tomorrow, then I will supply all your needs." Terry, believe me, I preached this in retreats, but I never believed it. I was living in the security of the Society of Jesus and all of that.

So what happened next? After a retreat this woman came and said, "Father, I enjoyed this retreat, and I really have trust, and I really saw Jesus when you spoke to us." Then she said, "Father, I think there is nobody else that can heal me, but you are going to pray to Jesus for me." I said, "Sure, Mary." Later, she called me on the phone. She was crying. She said, "I'm going to die, Father. I didn't tell you at that time, but I have a tumor, of cancer, right here on my head. . . . I'm losing my eyesight. Dr. Reeding is going to operate on me on Wednesday, and they say there is a seventy percent chance of death or paralysis. Father, please. . . ." She began crying. I said, "Mary, I'm going to offer the Mass and I'm going to pray for you. I'll say the rosary, and I'll. . . ." She said, "No, I'm going to come to the rectory and you're going to pray over me." "Mary, I can pray for you from here." "No, no, no, I'm going to come." So she came to the rectory and said, "Father, please put your hand over mine, on my head here." And I can see this tumor bulging by the side of her head. "Pray over me." "Mary, I don't do that!" I told myself that others can heal, Kathryn Kuhlman can heal, but I can't heal. And I told her we give the Last Rites, and the bishop confirms, but we don't heal. She said, "Father, please, Jesus did it, and he healed people. And I saw Jesus in you. You are his priest, and thanks to you, when you preached in that church, I experienced Jesus."

Now Mary is not in the Charismatic Movement at all. She's not Pentecostal; she never raises her hands and prays. But she prays the rosary daily for me.

Anyway, I put my hands on her. And you know what I say? The Sign of the Cross, the Our Father, the Hail Mary, the Glory Be, the Creed, the Hail Holy Queen, and I'm finished. And then I look at her and she's still waiting for the healing, and I can see that the tumor is not going down. So I say, "Lord, please heal Mary or she'll have no faith in me or in the priesthood. In her old age, you know. Please do something for her."

I think it was my own fears. I said, "Mary, there's a prayer group down here; the Lord is telling me that you must go there and they'll all pray over you." All I was saying was, you know, if I don't heal her they can share the blame with me. So she said, "No, I'm not going to go there. I know those people, hippies and all come there." So I said, "Mary, those people are people of God, and they're going to pray with you. I prayed already, but I think two or three must gather in His name." I was doing my own theory now.

So she went there with her husband. She was scared of these Charismatics, but she went out of obedience. Now, watch this obedience thing. And the people put their hands on her and they prayed. She got a shock through her body, and got so scared, she got up with her husband immediately after the prayer, and went home. I began to pray, "Please don't do her damage, just before her death, don't take away her faith." That was on Monday. Tuesday she went to the hospital; Wednesday, the operation was scheduled. She was not experiencing any pain. The doctors gave her an X-ray. The tumor had disappeared! There was no cancer!

Now this is on documentation. She's still living today. And she called me from the hospital. "Father, do you know what you have done to my life? You have healed me!" She was crying on the phone. I said, "Mary, I think it was all of us who prayed, not just me, okay?" I was happy to say that. But she said, "You healed me." And I said, "No, Jesus healed you, and you are going to go back to the prayer group, which you despise, and that you were so scared of, and you are going to praise God in front of them that you got healed. And you have to tell all the people what happened to you." "Sure, I'll tell the whole world, Father." She was crying then.

I was coming back from the airport in San Francisco once, and these friends came to greet me. And I hugged this woman, whom I really loved, and as I embraced her she got healed, without my praying for any healing. She had had a neck injury for years. I've never told this, by the way, to anybody. She went home and later told me, "Father, you know when you embraced me in love that night, in front of my husband, I got healed." I knew that I was ordained with power, that I could forgive sins, literally, but in a different way. I could heal people of their hurt. Now I had heard of the healing of memory, of literal healing of the emotions, which I was going to learn little by little, and this began my walk with God.

Sometimes people are not healed. I cannot understand the mysteries of God. Why he never healed some, I do not know. But I know that he heals others, and I know that he tells us to thank God even before they are healed. Before Jesus raised Lazarus from the dead, he said, "Father, I thank you and I praise you that you have answered my prayer." And then he said, "Lazarus, come forth." Father McNutt gives many theological reasons why people are not healed. Many do not heal others because they do not have compassion and love for the person they are healing. They are only treating him like a guinea pig, testing their failings of having faith.

Once, on a television show, I was moved to pray aloud for fathers of families, that they might be healed of any weaknesses they had. Months later, a man brought his wife and kids to see me. He told me he was an alcoholic for fourteen years.

He said, "Father, I must tell you something: I used to take half a tank like this of booze and just swallow it down, morning and night. I lost three good jobs as an engineer; I smashed up two cars; I used to land up vomiting on the road right in front of my house. I stopped my wife from going to Mass on Sundays, and I beat her and the childen. I had lost faith in God. I knew something was missing in me.

"One day I came into the house, turned on the TV, got my booze and my tobacco—I'm a chain smoker. So I'm turning the dial and I see this priest, and it was you. And you were praying for the fathers of families, and you said, 'Before you pray, all those who are now listening, put out your hands and touch the television set if you want the prayer to be good for you.' I never put out my hand, does he think I'm crazy? So, you began to pray for the fathers of families, for divorces, for alcoholism, and as soon as you said alcoholism, something happened and my hand was just forced to put itself on the television set. And no sooner had I put it there, than you said, in the name of Jesus, and bang! I fell on the floor. And I got up, and I had lost all taste for the booze. I had lost all taste for tobacco.

"Father, I wouldn't tell you if it was just immediate, just yesterday, but seven months have passed." So I asked, "What do you want me to do?" He answered, "Father, just one gift I want you to give me. You know, you brought me back to the faith of Jesus again. I've been going to prayer meetings. My wife is so happy. Here, my children, again, are smiling. I got back my job. I want to make my confession." I told him to come right in and took him to our little chapel, and I asked him to sit down. The Spirit was telling me, rejoice with this man because he who was lost has been found, who was dead has come back to life. And he began the confession. He went into his main faults, where he was hurting the most, where he had been hurt most by people, where he had never forgiven people, and it came out so beautifully. During the time for absolution, I put my hand upon him and I prayed for a healing. I had never done that before. I said, "Lord, heal him of his emotions." And I asked him what he wanted of the Lord Jesus. And he said, "I want the joy back that you have in your face, Father." And I prayed, "Father in heaven, in the name of Jesus, send this joy into my brother's heart which you have promised and said you would never refuse to your little ones, if they ask in the name of Jesus, especially if they ask for the Holy Spirit. And baptize him in the Spirit, Lord, and give him that joy." And believe me, Terry, I have never seen a guy . . . he was not pretending, he had come with a serious face, but now he was jumping up and giggling and laughing and was going through a powerful emotional experience. He said, "Father, you don't know the joy I have right now." I said, "It is because you've come home, that's why. You have come home, yes, but not to your Father in heaven. A banquet is made for you now as you go to the Eucharist. This confession is not the end of it. You are made to go to the Eucharist." I never knew this theology . . . I knew theology, yes, but not expressed this way.

And this man walked out and hugged his beaming child. He put her on the ground, and she came and hugged me. Now she was jumping like a little lamb. They went out to the street, got into the car, the child smiling at me, and drove off. And I said, "Praise you, Jesus, now you can take me to heaven, or take me wherever you want, you can let me die now. I have seen the power in the sacraments. And if I go on television, I'm not just going to tell the Pentecostal experience; I'm going to tell them about the power of the Eucharist again." Is there any other question?

SWEENEY: How do you think God looks upon you?

AFFONSO: I think God looks at me, and loves me so much I cannot even conceive it. I've taken that Scripture because it's so much in my heart, and that's how I think God looks at me. And I have experienced it: "Father, that they may all be one as you, Father, are in me and I in you, that the world may know that you sent me, and that you have loved them as much as you have loved me." Now that was inconceivable for me until I read the Gospel of John: "God loved the world so much that he sent his only begotten son to die." He died for me! Now I know what St. Ignatius is saying. For me! Now I know what that means, that he wrote a love letter to me in the Scriptures, that he wrote it in the lives of saints, and of every Christian that accepted him, and now he's writing it in my life.

Before, I had this intellectual knowledge of Jesus, now I experience the person of Jesus. And people say, I have experienced Jesus with you, I see Jesus in you. They never said it before. And I know it's not me. I know it is Jesus through me, now I know what Jesus said.

Who am I to Jesus? Jesus, I felt, has made me into himself, but a poor instrument who does not know where he's going. I feel so, so little. I feel like a child, like an instrument, like a loved one to a lover. And I feel that he loves me very much as a priest, that he called me to a very special vocation; and I wish this for any priest and bishop, that they may hunger now. Now I know what it is to be a saint. I am not proud when I say that he calls me to be a saint; he is making me into a saint now. I know there are thousands of saints around. I know you are a saint in the making. I am a saint in the making with different levels of experience of Jesus Christ. And I know that this is just the beginning.

This is how I see God looking at me. He says, "Hey, you, out there, you are nobody, and nobody loves you if I don't love you.

And if I didn't love you, you could not love anybody else either."
This has come so strongly to me. Before I used to love people
very passionately and lovingly. But they never came back to me in
that love. Now I feel that love is being fulfilled daily in my life
much more. Am I a sinner? Of course, I am a sinner. I get tempted,
I fall still, I'm struggling, I have my doubts in faith . . . but every
time I put them into his hands. . . . He wants me to praise and give
him that time because that is when he is molding me like gold in
the fire. And that is when he is making the stepping stones and
raising me higher. But I still experience it, and I pray for my
perseverance every day. But after having preached to all and
having recognized what sainthood is, I may lose it myself if I don't
rely upon my God. He makes me depend on him day by day by
day. That's what it is.

PHYLLIS DILLER

Wacky, zany, outrageous, riotously funny, unpredicta-
bly tender—some of the many adjectives used to
describe comedian Phyllis Diller.

SWEENEY: The first question I have is, who is God to you?

DILLER: Who is God to me? Well, let's put it this way: I don't picture God as a fellow with a beard. I picture God as a spirit. I picture God as a spirit in human beings while they're alive. The force for good in people while they're alive—I consider that God.

SWEENEY: And when that particular person dies, how does the Spirit of God continue? Or does it?

DILLER: Well, I believe only in whatever they have left behind in a spiritual way. I feel that when the body and the spirit's gone, then it's no longer there.

SWEENEY: How do you get in touch with this spiritual force inside of you or inside of other human beings?

DILLER: Well, spiritually. It's a thing that, see, while you're alive your mind is more or less of a transmitter. Of course it is electricity and you can telepathize. You can send messages without speaking, thought messages. And, prayer in another form could be called some form of hypnosis, hypnosis of others, or autohypnosis. In other words, you might pray to the God in you, that spirit in you.

SWEENEY: So, for you God is that spiritual energy in people, and does not extend or is not someone other than that energy within people?

DILLER: Well, let me explain. You see, everyone's idea of God and idea of religion is something that stems from birth. Now, you were obviously born a Catholic.

SWEENEY: Yes.

DILLER: Well, now if you are born into a Protestant home, and a Fundamentalist home, where you are spoon fed biblical fundamental religion, where you have, say, a parent who actually believes that there are silver and gold streets, and a guy, St. Peter, there at the gate with a horn, and there are people running around with feather wings. Now, even as a child, I couldn't buy that because I knew how uncomfortable the whole thing would be. I mean, I didn't want silver and gold streets. I mean, they'd be too cold or too hot, slippery, and I just couldn't see people with those big ugly wings—so I questioned my mother's fundamental religion.

SWEENEY: Was that Baptist or Methodist or . . . ?

DILLER: No, I have composite religions in my close background. I have many ministers in my background. I had a Southern Methodist minister, I had a Dunker minister, now that's the Friends, Quakers, all that sort of thing. You know those people?

SWEENEY: D-U-N-K-E-R?

DILLER: Dunker. It's one you never hear of . . . they're like Mennonites, Amish, those people.

SWEENEY: Oh.

DILLER: Those people dress that way, have beards, and wear those funny black hats, and the ladies keep their heads covered in the home. When they go out they wear a little black bonnet; when they're in the house, they wear a little white bonnet.

SWEENEY: What's the purpose of that?

DILLER: Don't ask me.

SWEENEY: So you were exposed to several different ministers?

DILLER: I was baptized a Lutheran, married a Presbyterian. I have been active in Presbyterian churches. I was active in churches back in California while I was musical director of the program for the young people, and for the ladies, and they put me in charge of their Mayday luncheon. It was the wrong time. It was the end of the war—the one before the last—and the ladies had decided that they wanted "songs of many lands" for the program. And I thought, great, because in this particular place where we were there was, really, one of everything. There were Mohammedans, Arabians, Japanese, Chinese, blacks, Italians, Polish, everybody.

And I thought, how terrific, we'll have each come, we'll put a show together, and have a. . . . Now, this was when I was a housewife, you understand. We'll have them singing in their native tongues and then in English. And, I'll never forget it at the meeting when we were coming into the final stages of planning this thing; when I proposed this, you would have thought I was going to stage it in a leper colony. And needless to say, they put the kibosh on it. That wasn't what they had in mind at all.

That was my last brush with organized religion.

SWEENEY: Right after the Second World War?

DILLER: Yep.

SWEENEY: What would you say were the major changes in your understanding of God, in your lifetime?

DILLER: Oh, well. I have a perfect understanding for me. It's personal and I wouldn't want to burden anyone else with it, but it works for me. You see, I see good in everyone. It's all a matter of percentages. There are some people who are ninety-nine percent good, and there are some people who are only one percent good. And if you use all the wonderful words like praise, bless, thank, love, you bring out the good and you raise that percentage in anyone you're dealing with. If you concentrate on the bad that will grow, because you constantly keep telling them about it.

SWEENEY: So if you focus on the really good and the virtuous, that is what is going to be developed in the other person?

DILLER: Well, I believe that.

SWEENEY: Yes, I do, too.

DILLER: I once had a maid who stole a diamond ring and I was sure that it was missing, but it never entered my head that she might have taken it. I guess I was sort of naive, but I would never have accused her. I know most people if there's anything missing, you know, the first person they're going to say took it . . . Anyway, you know, she brought it back.

SWEENEY: She brought it back?

DILLER: She brought it back, and put it right back where it was. That was the end of that. You see, if I had fallen into negative thinking, accused her or even mentioned it, or even let her think I thought. . . . But it never did cross my head.

SWEENEY: That's the power of positive thinking.

DILLER: . . . in action.

SWEENEY: Yes. Well, it seems that there would be quite a change between thinking of God as a person with a white beard, which is probably what you were raised in, to think of God. . . .

DILLER: Actually, it was brown. He was not old, he was young, or sort of a middle-aged person.

SWEENEY: Sort of middle-aged person after the model of Jesus, or some other . . . ?

DILLER: Well, everybody . . . when you think about God, who's going to picture what?

SWEENEY: Well, it depends on whom you're talking to, I guess.

DILLER: Well, what do you picture?

SWEENEY: When I think of God, I don't picture anything. But, when I think of Jesus, I have all kinds of different things that come to mind.

DILLER: Because he was a real person.

SWEENEY: Right.

DILLER: And we have art work of him.

SWEENEY: Right. No, when I think of God, there's no picture that comes into my mind . . . some kind of energy, or force of. . . .

DILLER: Well, I think that's what God is. It's the force, energy force for good.

SWEENEY: Do you still have some kind of understanding of God as being a person?

DILLER: Oh, my goodness, that's what I couldn't accept when I was six years old.

SWEENEY: Okay, so. . . .

DILLER: I never had that.

SWEENEY: Okay. For you God is the spiritual force inside of people?

DILLER: Yes. You see, when I was a child I had the thing of having parents who were as old as grandparents. Therefore, all their brothers and sisters were popping off, one a week; we belonged to a funeral of the week club. So, I went to all these funerals and it gave me reason to think, because they took little kids to funerals then, and they had them in their living rooms. And I touched a couple of stiffs . . . like my grandmother, for instance, and I had to think about those things; and I decided that her hereafter was in my mother and in me and would go on and on—what good she had planted.

SWEENEY: So really, God is kind of the force of good in people's lives.

DILLER: Yes.

SWEENEY: And the way that God survives is by continuing after death in the lives of those persons that are influenced?

DILLER: That's about it.

SWEENEY: Well, that's beautiful. That's very much the notion that a lot of Greeks had. That they would live on, their immortality was in terms of the memories that their children and grandchildren had of them, and that's why it was so important to live a virtuous life while they were alive. Because once they died that was it.

DILLER: I feel that, you know.

SWEENEY: Now, how would you answer the third question: who are you to God?

DILLER: Who am I to him?

SWEENEY: Yes.

DILLER: Him. Them. They. Well, I'm one of that Power's workers. I try to keep the percentage high, that's what I am to God. But, you see, "God" is a misleading word for what we're talking about.

SWEENEY: Yes, I know; that's why I'm going to put it in quotation marks.

DILLER: Yes, and it's a very misleading word to people because everybody has a different concept.

I woke up with great happiness one morning, and this thing just came to me—a thirty-four word prayer for world peace, which would be okay for school because it doesn't name any-body. Any person of any religion could say it. See, the minute you're a Catholic or a Democrat or a Chinaman you exclude a lot of people. You become part of a religion or an exclusive group. But I'm all for one and one for all.

JOE PASTERNAK

Joe Pasternak has produced 105 feature length films. He impressed me as being a happy man, very grateful to God for his family and successful career.

PASTERNAK: God is my partner. I admire him and respect him, and he guides me.

SWEENEY: And this understanding of God as your partner—what does this mean?

PASTERNAK: I pray to him at night, before I go to sleep. If I forget, I wake up. And then, I pray for him before breakfast. Of course, I'm looking for his kindness all the day through, and sometimes if I'm a little bit disappointed, I know he must have a reason. You can't expect him always to be on your side. But I feel that ever since I can remember, I made God my partner and he's always on the winning side.

SWEENEY: Is this relationship with God something that has really helped you in your work and your dealings with other people and has given you strength?

PASTERNAK: It gives me courage when I need it; it gives me strength when I need it, and when I am sick, he helps me get well.

I'll tell you a very funny story about God. I was doing the Deanna Durbin pictures at Universal. The gentleman at the gate called me and said there was a young lady who wanted to see me. So she came in and she said, "You remember wanting something really bad?" I said yes. She said, "I want very badly to interview Deanna Durbin." And I said, "Listen, everybody wants to interview. . . . I'll tell you something—there's a little church, Good Shepherd, on Santa Monica. Why don't you go over there and see who the movie stars are coming in, and interview them? Nobody

122

ever thought of them. Everybody thinks that motion picture people are sexy and all that stuff. We're basically very religious, most of us." So she thanked me. She went on Sunday morning to interview.

Anyway, she interviewed about six of them. She sent the interviews back to Detroit. They said they weren't interested in God; they were interested in scandals, so they fired her. So she came to see me, and I said, "All right, I'll hire you." And I hired her. She became a well-known writer. She started writing the next story for Deanna Durbin. Every time she sees me she says, "I'm very glad I made God my partner, thanks to you." She makes fifty thousand to seventy-five thousand dollars a year.

You'd be surprised how many famous stars you see in church thanking God. As long as they're with God they will be successful. About myself, I made one hundred and five pictures, and not one of them was classified "adults only." They were very successful, wholesome, clean pictures and found a great audience.

SWEENEY: One hundred and five motion pictures. Your career spans a long time.

PASTERNAK: I started working in the Paramount Studio commissary as a bus boy. I went through the ranks first as a second assistant director and then first assistant director. Then I was given the chance to go to Europe to produce for Universal since I was European and spoke German. I stayed in Europe for eight years. Hitler came to power and I came home. With God's help I was able to find that wonderful little girl, Deanna Durbin.

SWEENEY: In your lifetime has your understanding or your relationship with God changed?

PASTERNAK: No. I remember my faith when I was a youngster. You see, you can't find God if your father and mother haven't got it. My father was so religious. We were nine kids. He gave us a little bit of God, because that's all he had, but it was the greatest gift he ever gave me. And it's hard to understand it. God is in you. When I go to temple, I come out of there feeling like I took a clean shower. It's wonderful to have faith in something.

SWEENEY: Do you talk to God during the day?

PASTERNAK: No.

SWEENEY: Just in the evening before you go to sleep?

PASTERNAK: When I'm alone. As I say, before I go to sleep and when I wake up.

SWEENEY: And do you feel any kind of response from God when you pray?

PASTERNAK: Yes, because when I was ill, very ill, I got well. So somebody, it wasn't the doctor alone that did it, it was somebody we'd all like the doctor to know.

SWEENEY: When were you seriously ill?

PASTERNAK: . . . I had about four operations and survived all of them. So I had a good partner.

SWEENEY: You sure did.

PASTERNAK: I'm not selfish enough to pray just for myself. I pray for my family, for other good people, and for our country, our president. I hope you'll always be free to pray as you want to.

SWEENEY: Yes, me too. So, in terms of your lifetime there have not been any major changes in your relationship with God? The concept of God as partner has been pretty much your understanding?

PASTERNAK: Since I get older, I ask for more. You see, there's this terrible ordeal my folks went through in Europe with the Nazis. Seventy-two of our family were killed. My father was killed in a concentration camp, and my mother and my sister and six kids.

SWEENEY: Seventy-two of your family were killed during . . .

PASTERNAK: Both my mother and stepmother, my sister and six kids, my brother-in-law, my cousins, my uncles, seventy-two of them.

SWEENEY: How many of them were killed in the camps?

PASTERNAK: All.

SWEENEY: All! That's terrible!

PASTERNAK: Yes. . . . They say where is your God? I say, he must have a reason for it. Once in a while history reminds people when they go too far to the left they have to come back to the right.

SWEENEY: How do you think God looks upon you?

PASTERNAK: I hope, well, I hope he does. I know if I made a mistake I'd correct it. I say he's a very good partner and wants nothing when he gets old. I'm not friendly with him because I want things. I want to do something for myself, for him, for my wife.

SWEENEY: If I were sitting down having a conversation with God, and God were describing to me what he thinks of you, what do you think he would say?

PASTERNAK: He'd say, "He could improve."

SWEENEY: Improve?

PASTERNAK: There's always room to improve yourself.

SWEENEY: What else do you think he'd say?

PASTERNAK: He'd say I'm a lucky guy. I have been. I deserved it because I worked for it and I'm with him. I don't know. I don't talk too much. I always give him credit. I always understand when he does something. When you ask for a million, you know, you only get a hundred. He must have a reason for it. Because all are children of God, and I'm sure he doesn't think to hurt you, mislead you, or cheat you, or ruin you. He's always seeing you, the good things in you, I always feel. The bad things he forgives and the good things he remembers.

SWEENEY: Apart from the hospital experience, where you really felt that God cared for you and kept you alive, have there been other events when you really felt the hand of God?

PASTERNAK: You see, I came to America in 1921. I didn't know anybody. Nobody was helping me; but he guided me. He gave me ambition and he helped me. I can't put my finger on it—I came here a nobody but God was very good to me. I have a wonderful wife and three wonderful children and comfortable living. I didn't do it by myself. So I feel he had a hand in everything. I can't sing God's praises loud enough because there are so many things. You could fill a whole book.

SWEENEY: Well, I really appreciate this. I think that the activity of God in your life has been really extraordinary, and I think your faith in his being a partner is really beautiful.

PASTERNAK: I can only say, those fellows who don't believe in God are missing something wonderful. They shouldn't wait till they die to pray for it. As you get older. . . . That's wrong. You get older, you're not afraid of death. If you grow up with God, you're never afraid. Everybody fears the day will come. Nobody can get away from death. You're born, and you die. Especially, most of our movie stars. If they would have more faith in God, they wouldn't worry so much about getting older.

FRANK SULLIVAN

There are many people whose lives cross ours only briefly, and at unpredictable intervals. Over twenty years ago, while visiting a university classroom, I heard Frank Sullivan (Emeritus Professor and Thomas More Scholar at Loyola Marymount University) quoting Shakespeare with such feeling that I could not forget him. I was very pleased when he said yes to this interview. Frank died five months later.

SWEENEY: Who is God to you?

SULLIVAN: I don't think I belong in your book, because I feel that anybody who talks about God doesn't know anything about God. Talking about God is like talking about the pet names that you have for your wife. It's a very sacred and inner thing. It's impossible to talk about an experience like that.

To me, proving the existence of God is not important because everybody believes in God no matter what they say. They might call it chemistry, or five thousand years, or something similar. But they all believe in God. There is a force that produced these things—the uncaused cause.

But what's important to me about the uncaused cause is that the uncaused cause is interested in me, is approachable. That, as far as I'm concerned, is all there is to it. It seems to me that Aristotle, who was a reasonably intelligent man, didn't believe that God was interested. All right. There are many people who don't believe that God is interested. And there's no way you can prove that God is interested except by your personal experience. If I read St. Thomas Aquinas right, he never addresses himself to this question. He just sits down and at great length proves that there is an uncaused cause. Then he says, "which we call God." But I don't call that God.

Now, it seems to me that the big jump, the first big jump, is whether the uncaused cause is interested, has an interest whatsoever in me. When you look back over your life, carefully, you remember all kinds of moments when you felt God near you; when you felt that somehow or other you lucked out; when you got something you didn't deserve. If you can't smell a flower without worrying whether someone will think you're a homosexual, or if you can't put your arms around a tree and put your cheek up against it without worrying whether you're a cuckoo, or if you can't smell the ocean or walk on the beach at night, well then, you're never going to encounter these moments. But there are those moments when you can feel the springtime stepping up from Mexico, and all of a sudden you feel glad. And sometimes when you're in church saying your prayers, a great feeling of peace and love washes over you. So you file those things away. Well, then, later on you feel pain and sorrow and distress. And you think, well, I don't understand that, but I'll wait for that smell of the springtime and that touch of the bark of the tree or the sound of the sea in the moonlight, and when it comes it will come.

So this is what I think of God. But some people are more concerned with the question, is the uncaused cause interested in me only to pick on me? For thousands of years, people have felt that the uncaused cause was kind of, you know, seeing how much difficulty he could give. So you threw your kids into the fire, and you sacrificed virgins, and you did all kinds of stupid things. And then in the Christian era you beat yourself up or you fasted, or something like that. Not that I'm objecting to fasting. I'll talk about that in a minute. But people have made themselves miserable in order to get the uncaused cause to pay attention to them. Now, this, I think, is a lot of horseshit. Don't edit the word horseshit. Because that's the only word that will go.

Now, I've written about love in which I say it's an appetite to possess the good. I think that the kind of people I just mentioned love God, want to possess God, in the sense that they want to control him. You know, they say the seven little sermons of

Blessed Baxter of Boniface or some damn thing, and all of a sudden they are going to get what they want.

When I was a kid there used to be a real screwball devotion to St. Rita. No matter what it was, you asked St. Rita. She'd give it to you. But then, Ker-pow! She'd punish you for asking, you know. And so, no matter what it was, you were going to get it. If you wanted to pass your examinations, you prayed. You passed your examinations, and your mother dropped dead. And this was the cult of St. Rita. She charged. But you went to her, but she got to be too expensive. I don't think anyone goes to St. Rita now.

And then you had the cult of . . . dozens of them. What else did we have? Miraculous medal and Lady of Perpetual Help. You went every Tuesday to the Rock Church in St. Louis, where they kept the colored people out; and, if you went *every* Tuesday, then zingo! You were going to get it.

That's an attempt to possess God the way you possess your automobile. You pour in the gasoline and you turn it on and it goes. Here you pour in the penitential act and then God gives you what you want.

Well, that isn't the way you possess your wife or your husband. You possess your wife or your husband by kind of merging into them so that their happiness is your happiness, their sadness is your own. And this gives you a feeling of strength.

To return to the business of fasting: you make yourself hungry, not because God wants you to be hungry, but so that you can participate in the hunger of other human beings. I don't know what it's like to be in jail. I couldn't possibly know. There's no possible way I can understand what it's like to be in Vietnam. But I can understand hunger. And I can put myself into this situation of hunger. I can say, "God, this is so I'll understand my fellow men and I'll love my fellow men and I'll understand what's there." When I put flowers on the altar it isn't because I think God needs flowers. It's because I need to give God flowers.

The lesser creatures you possess by controlling them; human people, you possess by merging with them. And you possess God by disappearing. By just simply losing yourself in God. That's why it always sounds so phony when somebody starts telling you what God is to them, because the only way you can get to God is to get completely outside yourself, and this is a very difficult thing to do. God knows I don't do it. I'm not a pious person at all. But, as I said, I am convinced by my great personal backlog of what you might call incredibly good luck. And that includes, you know, right up to now when they tell me I have cancer. So, I'd rather not have cancer, but I don't see anything outrageous about it. I don't see why I should stand around and say, "Why me?" I say, "Why not me?" That's just one of those things. And it isn't that I'm brave. You know, when it gets bad I'll be screaming and hollering for the needle just like anybody else. But until that comes I just can check off the moments of great gladness that I have in the presence of God.

St. Thomas says that the thing you know, you become. So by trying to know something about God, in a kind of way you become a part of God. That may sound on the edge of heresy; but as you go back over all the good luck in your life, and you see that God is interested in you, and you know there is a certain affection for you, then you begin to get closer and closer to God and lose yourself more and more inside him.

If I wanted to summarize the one thing I wanted to say, it would be that *everybody* believes in God, no matter what they say, in the sense of the uncaused cause. The point where the loving Christian parts company with the materialist, atheist, the evolutionary character, is that the loving Christian thinks that this uncaused cause is interested; and you can't prove that with logic, but only by experience. It seems to me you learn to love God by putting together a great anthology of your goodness and gladness. And I know there are lots of saints who have loved God by putting together an anthology of their miserableness. Lots of people don't have time to think about God. Lots of people get scared when they think about God. They have the idea that God is out to get them. And they have a kind of feeling that if they don't talk about it, maybe he won't notice them.

You know, the great *hubris*: the minute you attract the attention of the gods, they slap you down. Well, that's why they don't talk about God. They're afraid of him. You've heard the saying, "Fear of the Lord is a virtue"; and they go out of their way to explain what Fear of the Lord is.

What I'm trying to say is, I think there are two routes to spirituality. One is, you concentrate on your ugliness and your evil and your sinfulness and ask God to pardon you. I don't like that particularly. I like St. Ambrose's idea that man is certainly a marvelous thing, an incredible thing. Like King David, dancing and stripping and singing before the Ark of the Lord. David and I identify, boy, do I identify. He's a dancer, and a singer, and a shouter. Oh, David I love.

SWEENEY: What difference does it make to you that God is interested?

SULLIVAN: Well, if he isn't interested, I'm in a helluva fix. My big temptation—normally I don't talk about this—is to worry about his lack of interest. That's my big temptation. I don't mean temptation in the sense that it's a destructive thing. It's just—the idea that he might not be interested in me—I can't look at that. It tears the guts out of me. I've written a poem about temptation, about how I have this fear, this cancer in my heart.

　　And then with Easter sunrise sorrow
　　　　sets God's grace
　　a cloak of sarcenet around my heart.

Sure, it makes a big difference to me.

JULIE BADEN

Extremely active in the Charismatic Movement, Julie has the constant challenge of balancing her home responsibilities with what she feels is her privilege to witness, teach, pray, and proclaim Jesus. This interview reveals something of the spirit that moves her life.

SWEENEY: Who is God to you?

BADEN: Right now, can I just pray with you for a minute?

SWEENEY: Sure.

BADEN: Just to see what the Lord would like me to say at this time. . . . Our Father, strengthen my flesh now, let us seek your understanding, take the distractions out of my mind. Father, send the Holy Spirit to use me right now to speak to my brother for whatever purpose he has for this book. We ask you to bless the whole book and whatever small part that I have in touching another heart and turning it to you. And use me now for the praise and glory of your name. Amen.

Okay, I guess, it sounds so crazy if I were to ask who is God to me. He's just everything. He's you, he's my dog, he's the tree outside . . . he's even like the chair I sit on; it's like the totalness of everything, you know, the whole world to me is God. There just isn't anything that I touch or see or feel before me that is not God. I guess maybe when I see him in so many things, I just can't look at anything—there was a time that I could—and take it for granted. I can't even look at something like a carving on the back of a chair without thinking of God. I just all of a sudden am so impressed; if you ask me what impressed me the most, it's that some human being could do that. It's like God builds, it's like my God is so great that it seems to me he built the whole world just to serve me. He built the whole universe just so I could sit on this chair. I mean, it's crazy you know, sometimes it's almost an awareness of how many people are involved in my life every day to make me comfortable. When I go in the refrigerator to get a glass of milk, I'm so aware that somebody placed that milk in there, somebody else took care of the cow. There's whole communities of people serving, and I'm getting the benefit of their service. And then I think this is how great my God is that he would have done all this for me. Even to look at a picture on the wall, God created someone to put that picture there. So God's in that picture, and I can look at it and enjoy something.

God is like the performance of everything. All of creation comes to life because God is in it.

I feel such a dependency on him because I'm aware that anything beautiful that's been in my life is because God is in it. And I find, even today, it just doesn't seem to matter what happens, I really understand the words of Scripture where it says God can bring good out of evil for those who love him. If you love him, there's just no evil in the world. It's just like evil is a stepping stone to being drawn closer to God. Like my boy being on drugs—I can say his being on drugs was the greatest place where God brought us into a relationship. I did not have a relationship with my boy until he was on drugs, until he got into a desperate situation, until I became a desperate mother, until I knew I couldn't cope with it. I turned to my God and then, again, I saw the hand of God as he brought Bobby and me into such a beautiful relationship through suffering. If you ask me if I was miserable, yes, but I learned how to pray. I learned that prayer is so simple it escapes us. It's not a form, it's not a bunch of words. Sometimes God has put prayers in my heart that are beautiful. I'm listening, they're beautiful, they're poetic, they're inspiring, and I get uplifted, and find myself soaring up to heaven with God. And I say, "God, how you can give me a prayer like this?"

And at other times the prayer is so desperate it's just, "help!" you know, "help, God, I need something." It's a desperate cry. But it's in the desperate prayer from my heart that I have found the greatest closeness to my God. I almost prefer the suffering to the moments of too much rejoicing, because even in that rejoicing I'm caught up in myself again having a good time. Like, my daughter Susan was picked up by police and put in a mental institute. Hearing her shout four letter words, cussing me out and calling me names . . . I knew God had showed me so clear then that this was not my daughter speaking, this was another force. Loving her completely. I knew that God gave me the love, so I knew again that God answered a prayer. I didn't have to say the prayer, God gave it to me. Right on the spot God gave me a discernment of the spirit that was hovering over me, and I saw Sue and her suffering. I saw who was controlling her, and God not only gave me the prayer in my heart, he gave me the confidence that he was going to handle this. When she was brought to that position, Sue had not spoken to me for over a year. She couldn't stand me, she couldn't be near me. Six months earlier she had been diagnosed schizophrenic. She ran away from UCLA hospital and the police picked her up and brought her to St. John's.

When I went into St. John's Hospital the Lord told me really clear, "I'm going to teach you something today. Perfect love casts out all fear." And I walked into Susan's room. They had her tied down and she wasn't responding. They told me she wasn't speaking to anyone, she was real hostile. But her face looks up, and she says, "Hi, Mom." And I say, "Hi, Sue." And she grabbed me and pulled me down on the bed! And she just clung to me, you know, and the attendant said, "You're not allowed to do that." So I sat down on the chair and Susan sat up, fell into my arms and hugged me even though she was strapped in from the waist down. She said, "Mom, why was I born?" And I said, "To know, love, and serve God and to be happy with him." And she said, "I want to be happy, but I just can't . . . I'm so afraid, I'm so afraid." And I said, "Honey, we're just going to rebuke that spirit of fear because it's not going to be with you. Jesus has taken over now." And she straightened up. It was just like somebody had shot her with a bolt and she looked at me. She kept staring at me so long I felt conscious of it, and I turned, and she said, "Don't turn away from me, I have to look into your eyes." And I said, "Why?" And she said, "I have such a peace when I look into your eyes. I just got this peace, just sit there, Mother." So I did, and we just stared at each other. But there was this love I cannot describe, Terry. It was flooding me from head to toe and I . . . it was just like I couldn't stop and it was just like . . . it was every bit of compassion for her, every bit of love for her. And the words came to me at that point, "Could you love her if she's like this always?" And, I had so much love, I said I could love her no matter what. The whole world hated her. I loved that girl more than anything in the world, I said. I'll never stop loving her, I said. And just as I was saying it, just when I loved her so much, that's when God healed her.

God showed me that you've got to love a person when they ask because that love is the power which restores them. And as I sat there, I really praised God with my heart's contentment. I knew God had taken over. I knew that every kind of independence had been shattered. When I couldn't do anything, he took over. And that's when he answers my prayer, when I am so helpless. And he took Susan and me in the month and a half—maybe it was a mental hospital to everybody else—but to me, it was a chance to be with her every day. There was no way for me to be with Sue before because she was on her schedule and I on mine. She was too busy before, you know, and we couldn't have gotten together. She couldn't stand me. And now, she was a captive audience, and I was a captured mother. He gave us one and a half months to visit together every day. It was only ten minutes, but we were both stuck with each other, and at the end of that month and a half she said, "I've got to come with you, I just love you so much." And she said, "I never knew how much I loved you." And, Terry, we are so close that no person could take that away, no person. And that, you know, in a sense is what God means to me. He's just every-thing—I don't even know where to start or where to finish—it's every single act every day. It's so beautiful, and it's a prayer life that you live. It's prayer. The whole day is a prayer.

SWEENEY: When did you come into this very strong sense of God's presence?

BADEN: When I got married I was close to God. I think all my life, Terry, I prayed a lot. My father was kind of unsteady and my mother . . . I remember as a little kid I was always on my knees praying for my parents, praying for my sister. I was the youngest of six kids. Always liked praying, just seemed like I was always praying for everybody. When I was in Catholic high school, I was kind of a rebel because if I didn't believe something, I just couldn't take it. Always questioning, seeking answers, looking for God.

When I had the babies I don't think I would have done anything like people told me, use contraceptives. I was at death's door four times. I had a very serious hemorrhaging problem when I had my babies, and so it was always a matter of life or death. And then every year I would find out I was pregnant again. I mean, it just was so crazy what God was doing to me in those eight years. But I never had a sense that I was going to die. Or if I did, it didn't matter, you know. I had such a perfect peace when I was pregnant. I had such a perfect love for my babies. And friends who would see me after I had a baby would say, "Wow, I just don't see how anybody could be that slim." God never destroyed any muscle in my body. He kept me like the same weight before and after. I'd go right back into my clothes. I could go back on the tennis court or whatever I was doing. I don't know. He just took care of me.

But it was not an experience of God. I had a lot of faith in him, but it was like God was far away. You know, it was like if someone had said use a contraceptive. No, I'm not going to do it. Use rhythm, I'd try it; okay, it doesn't work. I could accept God's ways, but I did not know that God had a plan for me. I really thought that you lived life out like you planned it. You have to plan your life; you don't bother to see if God had already something planned for you. I was making the plans, you know, I was running the show, really.

And, then, my son Bob was born with a severe hole in his heart. And they told me that it was chronic, he'd have to have surgery in a year, and there was nothing to do about it. Well, he was my sixth child, the fourth boy, and I was crushed because, you know, I pictured this little baby sitting on the sidewalk while the other boys were playing football, or baseball, and my heart just cried out for him in the hospital. And I remember then the prayer was so clear, I'm sure the Lord put it in my heart. I said, "I'm a mother, you know, dear God. I'm a mother and people say accept this, but a mother can't accept anything but a perfect child, she can't. Give me a hole in the heart, fine, you want to do it to me, but I want that baby healthy. I want him healed because I said that's the job of

a mother to see that her kids are healthy, and well taken care of."
The boy was miraculously healed in three weeks. The doctors
could find no hole in his heart.

Mary was very close to me. I prayed to her more than anyone
else, but I had no form to my prayer life because I had a terrible
memory. I could never memorize a prayer. And still, to this day, I
can't memorize. Even the prayer the "Our Father"—I'd say it
backwards halfway through sometimes. So I had to pray in my
own way, just talk to God.

You ask how did I meet him. Through my life he really has
shown me great gifts, like my seven kids. Do you know they never
had an antibiotic shot until they were about sixteen years old?
Never had a sick child. I never even knew God was doing all that
for me. I really sort of lost the pattern of him. You know, off to the
tennis courts. He became further away, till four years ago. Then I
had that experience with Jesus. For the first time the whole
picture reversed.

SWEENEY: Would you describe that experience?

BADEN: Okay. After having the babies, there were ten years when
I played tennis, bridge, and socialized a lot more, and I felt great. I
had a lot of friends; I've always had just loads and loads of friends.

Then I got a call from this little Sister Ignatius and she said,
"Would you come to this prayer meeting that we're having
tonight? Maybe you'd enjoy coming with your husband." She was
such a sweet nun that I said, "If my husband wants to come
tonight, we'll come." My husband said he'd love it. So we ended
up on a Monday night praying with Sister Ignatius.

The feeling I had was almost like the years that I had the babies.
I wasn't aware that this prayer group had the Gift of Tongues, I
wasn't aware of anything like that. I just had the feeling of being
close to God again, and it was a quietness that I used to have when
I was pregnant and had the little babies, and loved them. I felt that
I had come home to something but I couldn't describe it.

Thursday of that week my sister called me—she had four little
babies, her oldest was eleven, her little one is three—and she
said, "I'm going to die." And I said, "I don't know what you're
talking about." And she said, "I'm going to tell you this really fast,
Julie, if I don't, I won't have the courage to tell you anything. I've

already had cobalt. I went to my doctor for a regular Pap smear, and they discovered cancer." And I told her that I'd heard of people cured. And she said, "It's not that kind; they only discovered it here by accident. The cancer is moving so fast it's just a matter of a month."

This is a sister who, you know, all my life I've done everything with that I've ever done. God really blessed me because I would have been saying I know this doctor and this doctor but I said, "Betty, I know a prayer group, and I remember somebody saying that they had prayed for someone and they got healed. I'm going to go right down there next Monday and I'm going to pray for you." She said, "Well, thanks, Julie, I'd really appreciate it, you know." So the following Monday I went back to Sister Ignatius, but this time I was desperate! I sat down and listened! I wanted to hear everything, what had happened here and what had happened there, and who'd been healed; and I waited for the cancer cures to come and somebody had a cancer cure and they told about it; and the meeting was over, and the tears were coming down and I said, "Would you pray? My sister is going to die." And, what a beautiful bunch! They rallied around me and one of the men has the Gift of Healing. They said, "Don't worry, Julie, you're going to sit in the chair and we're going to pray over you." And the prophecy came, "Your sister's been healed." I sat there in seventh heaven, and Betty Graf—you never forget the one who prays over you for your Baptism—put her hand on me and said, "Would you like the Baptism of the Holy Spirit?" She might just as well have said, would you like to go to Timbuktu, because I didn't even know what the words meant! And I said, "Listen, anything God wants to do to me!" Inside, I said, "This isn't for me, Lord, don't you let them touch me." I sat there waiting to see what was going to happen; and well, everything happened! I felt this vibration going through me and I was really amazed. Then someone said, "You have the Gift of Prophecy. Speak." And I said, "I don't have anything to say. I'm all confusion." Someone asked, "Do you have the Gift of Tongues, Julie?" And I said, "I don't have." And I sat there and I don't know what they were talking about, really. Finally they said, "Just say anything, the Lord's speaking to you." And I said, "Well, he doesn't want me to say anything. I've nothing to say." But I got drunk in the Spirit, Terry . . . Now for having been so low about my sister, I was just completely drunk in the Spirit.

By the next day—I can't explain—it was like my whole body was washed clean, like somebody had come and just scrubbed me. I could feel the sanctification of the body like the Lord had just washed me clean like a little kid. I had such a love experience that I couldn't relate to my husband and children. I can't describe it, you know. I told someone once that if you could speak in the Spirit, you could talk about this experience. I knew then, so clear, how the Blessed Mother could have been a virgin and how she would never have had to have sexual expression—because it was so immaterial in my life. I mean, it was like I had been just completely raised to a love level that excluded any desire for that. It's an incredible thing to explain, and I don't know how to explain it. I only know it was. I only know that after that I didn't care to go out, and I was a person who went out all the time. My greatest joy was to go in my bedroom, sit down and listen as Jesus spoke to me. And I could write things, I could write Scripture. He spoke my whole life to me. He began to lead me and it was just one to one. And then my greatest thing became to hurry and get everybody out so I could be with him. Now, I don't know why he was in my bedroom, but it was just like that's all I wanted. I didn't even hunger to go to a prayer meeting, as some people would, except to hear something exciting was happening. But the thing for me was two months of wanting to be in my bedroom, not to read books, but to be listening. And he was speaking continuously. I began to write what he was saying to me, and I just knew things. It just seemed I knew things that Fr. Victor had to study to learn. I began to write and give it to him. It fascinated him because he'd say, "Did you study this?" "Nooo. . . ." And he'd say, "Did you read it?" And I said, "No." But then as I began to take the Scripture out, it was like I knew everything that was in there. It had all been revealed to me prior to even opening the Scripture. So I realized that you could be illiterate, you didn't have to own a Bible, and it could already be in your heart. There's so many things that you know that are in your life already and you never even realize until you turn on the Spirit.

I walked up Santa Monica Boulevard, and I just never saw such beautiful things. The buildings were beautiful—they're ugly buildings, right? I said, "Why is everything so beautiful?" I was just wiped out. I said, "I know I'm crazy. But I don't want to be any different. I want to stay in this crazy way and let the whole world be sane if that's what they are, but let me be crazy." And that's the way I felt. And yet prayer was still just talking to God. I could just pour my heart out. Jesus would tell me so much about himself. He said he knew all about me and I knew that he knew. I was just so hungry to know about Jesus and how he felt about the church. And I found myself saying, "Okay, how do you feel about Mass?" And he told me, and I wrote it down and gave it to Victor. It was like Jesus said, "You are really hurting me with the Mass." And Victor said, "What do you mean?" And I said, "Well, we insult him by making the Mass under pain of mortal sin." And he spoke it so clear to me: "Julie, how do you feel when you have a dinner party and your guests are forced to come?" I said, "I hate it." He said, "How do you think I feel at my dinner party when man puts laws to force people to come? I created them free. Nobody should have put them under pain of sin." Well, I was crying and I wanted to tell the whole world. I wanted to go in the pulpit and say, "Listen, stop what you're doing. Why are we hurting him? What is this banquet? Why aren't people coming freely? Do you think it's because Jesus is such a bad host? No," I said, "it's because you put on such a bad party for him. When I throw a party at my house, I try to make it so interesting that people are ringing the door wanting to come. Why don't you do the same for Jesus? Why don't you take the time to make it beautiful?" I said. "When you have a school carnival, you knock yourself out for every detail. Do you knock yourself out or do you just go through the motions of the liturgy?"

These are the things that Jesus and I talked about. I was excited. I mean, I couldn't wait to just go see what he had to tell me. The prayer felt so different; it was like getting in touch with him, and that's where my whole life changed. You ask where was the difference: Instead of asking the Lord to do things for me, it was like being in love.

It's hard to say what is prayer. I think prayer is really being in union with someone; it's communicating in perfect oneness. I can take no for an answer from him without having to understand because I know he loves me. He's made himself so clear to me that he loves me, that if he said no, I'll go back and ask him for the same thing two days later. It's like this: I've said no today to my kids, but I know that if they ask me the same thing a week later and the circumstances have changed, I'll say yes. God is like that.

In prayer God gave me so many teachings. For two months it was parable after parable of my own life in relation to what he wanted of me. He would just teach me. He said, "Now you know, Julie, take your two youngest kids. You've given them both a tricycle, and they're out in front, and you say, please don't ride on the street, it's dangerous. So you give them these little guidelines. One child will do it and you never worry about that child. But the other one, as soon as he gets on that tricycle, goes in the street every time. You finally take the tricycle away, you put him in the house and you stand him in a corner. Which do you love the most?" And I say, "I love them both." He said, "I, too, love them both. I really want all of you out there participating, walking into the kingdom freely, just coming in and out; but you've got to know the territory by which you come and go. You've got to know the boundaries that are for your own good. When you learn obedience to me, you're free."

Now this is true freedom. I know my God loves me so much I cannot commit a sin that he won't forgive. It's an impossible thing because he's just like I am to my children. Even if my kids commit murder tomorrow, I'm still at their side, I'm their mother. I would love them, and I know it. They can't do a thing that would break my relationship. That's how I know how my Father is. I can't do anything to break the relationship between God and me. If I want to walk away, I can walk away, I'm free. If I stay away twenty years, then decide to go back, he takes me. Just like the prodigal son. So what happens? In that freedom I never want to go away. Because I'm free to sin I don't even want to sin.

You ask what is God. He is so forgiving. If I could give that message to people, they'd never have a hangup. They wouldn't even care if they did. If they committed a hundred million murders, I could say, so what? He died for a hundred million murderers, individually. Like the statement that Jesus would die if I was the only person on the face of the earth. I really learned the meaning of that just very recently. He meant that if everybody was going to sin and abandon him except one person, God would have gone through the whole act. The whole act!

SWEENEY: What happened to your sister?

BADEN: Oh, she did die. I'm sorry I got off that track. But anyway, she was healed completely, Terry, at that time. Completely. The doctors could not find a cancer in her body. She died a year later.

SWEENEY: Of what?

BADEN: Cancer. It came back a year later. But she was completely sanctified. She was so beautiful that my prayer when she died was, Lord, take her. I really was jealous of her because I would have liked to have gone where she was going. At her funeral I felt such joy. I had the four little ones and all the kids were there, and I was at perfect peace. It was the craziest thing. Like in a special way we were placed in God's hands. When she died it was like St. Stephen's death, like I saw heaven open up, and she walked right in without any suffering at all. I can't describe it. These are mysteries, and I don't know how to explain how I can feel so confident that my sister is with the Lord.

JOHN VASCONCELLOS

In 1969, John Vasconcellos, Assemblyman for the Twen-ty-third District in California, gave a talk to a Jesuit High School faculty on the dehumanizing effects of an education that develops only the cognitive powers of students. He criticized at length his heavily intellec-tual Jesuit training and concluded his talk with a challenge to the Jesuit faculty to expand its educa-tional methods and provide a learning environment in which the affective dimensions of the students could be expressed and developed. His address was straight-forward, honest, personal. I expected he would be the same in talking about God.

SWEENEY: My recollection of what you said during our dinner conversation about God was that even the term doesn't have much meaning.

VASCONCELLOS: It lacks meaning for me. The phrase has no presence operationally in my life. I don't think about who or what God, or church, or religion is for me personally, except when somebody asks me like this.

SWEENEY: For you none of these have meaning—God, church, religion, faith?

VASCONCELLOS: Well, none except "faith." "Faith" is important for me. But its meaning is totally new and different. I have faith in myself, in my own humanness, and faith especially in the struggle to let myself go, to release myself from constraint, oppression, guilt, and the sense of sin I was raised with and lived with for a long time. These things kept me away from my own being, from my natural decency. They were literally anti-"faith" in myself.

142

I suppose whatever people live by is what religion is about and what God is about. What I live by is a sense of my own basic, inherent trustworthiness and my struggle to open up to that, to myself.

SWEENEY: Before, you mentioned three different people whom you had talked to. Was there anything in their various answers that struck you?

VASCONCELLOS: I told one close friend I was going to see you and discuss who God is for me. He said, "Well, who is God for you?" I answered, "Well, I guess it's me and you and the other people whom I care about." A second friend said that somehow God represented a collective second coming where we each and all recognize our own being God-like, and become open to that recognition and really get ourselves together. A third friend said that God has to do with recognizing and realizing the best that is in us and between us—our human potential.

SWEENEY: This gets back to your use of the term "faith." Am I understanding it correctly to say that "faith" for you means to be faithful to what is most fully yourself and to discover who you are?

VASCONCELLOS: Yes. With a belief, an intellectual belief, that at root depths I am good, trustworthy and caring, and thereupon struggling towards (discovering) my own faithfulness; and more recently, emerging from that struggle, a deepening experience of my own inherent faithfulness.

SWEENEY: You've probably heard the terms "transcendence" and "immanence." God is "transcendent" and God is "immanent." I know that you're saying that he's not "out there" and he's not that other reality. And you're also saying that he's not "in here."

VASCONCELLOS: I just don't know. I guess all I know is that there *is* an "is" in here. You know? In me, and in you. My life is about trying to open up the connection with (in) myself, and the connection between myself and other persons. I told you earlier that if I were rationalizing my position intellectually, it would be that if there is a God, he would want me to live the way I'm living, which is attempting to be open, authentic, and loving. But I don't think I rationalize. It just doesn't occur to me. Your God doesn't have any immediacy for me. He has no meaning, doesn't touch me. As I told you earlier, I don't *know* whether I'm overreacting to thirty-five years of living largely a lie in the sense of church and God and authority and guilt, or whether I'm just simply in a place where that has no meaning for me. I don't know, but I'm pretty sure I'm living my own place and not just still reacting.

SWEENEY: That leads very naturally to the second question which is: How has your relationship with God changed over the years?

VASCONCELLOS: For thirty-five years I was a liberal but very traditional Roman Catholic. When I came back from the Army overseas and started law school at age twenty-four, I went to Mass every morning at six-thirty. When they switched from Latin to the English Mass, I opposed that. The Catholic Church and religion were a central motivating belief system: that was what I lived by. But eventually I found that I couldn't any longer live by that, and that I wouldn't.

SWEENEY: Also one of the things we talked about before dinner was God and guilt—how much your concept of God is tied up with a . . .

VASCONCELLOS: So much. And probably so long as I have some of that guilt in me, that connection would still be present. I spend a lot of energy and a lot of pain and therapy, with myself and in relationships, struggling with the whole issue of guilt: the presence in me of guilt about my own feelings, my sexuality, my body, impulses, and desires. I grew up in a traditional Catholic family. My parents have been married forty-nine years, had three kids, and still go to Mass every day. I lived a torment of fear and guilt and shame for so long and in so many ways. That came from the home, from church, and from schools—public till high school, then eleven years of Jesuit training. So guilt, church, religion, and God were all tied up. And I just don't want to be part of that any longer. I don't think it's healthy; it kept me for so long from being myself.

SWEENEY: Was there ever a time in the past when your sense of God was more expansive than your sense of guilt and authority?

VASCONCELLOS: Well, the church began to change. There was a lot of talk and music about "God is love" and all that, which was very appealing to me intellectually. But I wasn't really able to feel that. Intellectually it had meaning, but I had pretty much locked the rest of myself away. I gather there has been a lot of change in the church about what God is.

But one of the experiences that led me towards recognizing that I was leaving the church came after a retreat I made in Santa Cruz in '63. It was a very intimate and personal experience, ten persons who were friends, going to Mass and praying together with the priest. The next day was a holy day. I went to Mass in the Sacramento cathedral. There were a thousand people, it was impersonal and unfulfilling. There was no feeling of presence. I recognized that kind of religion was no longer of any use to me.
SWEENEY: Now, this particular event that you are referring to of going into the Sacramento cathedral with a thousand people—was that kind of *the* turning point? Or was it just something that gradually took place over many months?
VASCONCELLOS: Oh, I guess it came gradually, over a year and a half. That was one piece of it, a moment of recognition. A more powerful piece was getting involved in a deep relationship. I'd always been very stiff and contained, very alone and aloof from people. Then I got involved in a powerful, shattering relationship and found myself experiencing emotion and feeling and love and sexuality in ways that I hadn't before then. It was so obviously healthy and good that the whole "police system" that was the church didn't make sense and couldn't help anymore.

That challenged my belief in sin, especially "original sin." I don't believe in original sin anymore. That's a terribly destructive self-fulfilling prophecy we put on ourselves and on each other from day one. We assume the newborn infant is basically evil, and then we proceed to edit him (her) and repress him, we touch him coldly and tell him not to act or be himself. The effect is profound: what begins as good gets distorted, what is innocent becomes guilty.

Another piece was one day I realized I didn't agree with and no longer could say "Oh, Lord, I am not worthy." Then I realized I just didn't belong in the church, because one of its more basic tenets in its most sacred ritual was utterly foreign to my sense of who I was. The church really constrains you with that dogma.
SWEENEY: At least the way you're describing that religious relationship in the past, one of the senses that emerges from your

description is that you almost identified or equated God with church, or God as church. Is that accurate?

VASCONCELLOS: That's probably accurate. It just utterly pervaded me. God, religion, and church owned all of me.

SWEENEY: So in a way, what no longer has any meaning for you is God as church, God as moral authority?

VASCONCELLOS: That's correct. But even more, when you ask the question, "who is God to me," I have utterly no idea of who God is or would be or could be.

What is truly meaningful for me in my life now is the experience of my own trustworthiness. These are the most profound moments of my life now. They have nothing to do with any sense of God I recalled ever having. These occur in relationships with other humans. (Two particularly . . . one male, one female . . . come to mind.) In their presence I've experienced a feeling of total safety and total innocence and being totally trusted. What is more beautiful for me now is wanting to be trusted in ways that leave me expanding and more free and unafraid and discovering knowledge and wisdom I didn't know I had.

These experiences most nearly approach whatever it was that I used to think God was, a mystical or religious experience. I observe myself increasingly open to my own self and my feelings and intuition. Occasionally I meet someone and just flash some sense of desire or attraction and trust and involvement. I'm freer now to trust and reveal my feelings, and I occasionally find there's an identical or reciprocal experience in the other person, and a truly healthy, powerful, and empowering relationship ensues. That's what I know that comes closest to the intellectual concept I used to have of God as love. I feel whole and free, safe and unafraid, innocent and tender and loving.

SWEENEY: Is it correct to say that your understanding of God in the past was so much tied up with things like authority, commandment, institution, sin, guilt, fear, and shame that to be related to God was precisely the thing that was keeping you from being yourself?

VASCONCELLOS: Yeah. That all meant self-denial, self-sacrifice, and self-surrender to and for me. And despite the church changing from a God of fear to a God of love, that didn't reach the roots in me of all that debilitation I had earlier taken in. I simply had to break out and leave, leave it all behind me.

SWEENEY: So the God in your past is the God who kept you from loving and from discovering yourself.

VASCONCELLOS: Yes.

SWEENEY: I'm glad you got rid of him.

VASCONCELLOS: So am I. I've mostly gotten rid of him intellectually in my head. But I still carry deep traces of him in me emotionally and in my body. But I believe I've turned a corner and passed the point of no return. I'm now actively, faithfully, into my own daily growth process and I am finding myself more and more clear, immediate, authentic, and open to relationships.

SWEENEY: It strikes me that your experience in a way articulates and sums up the experience a lot of people have had with the church, except they haven't pushed it to the degree you've pushed it—or been pushed, depending on how you look at it.

VASCONCELLOS: I just had to do it. One day I just got so isolated that I just crashed through it out of necessity. I was fortunate in meeting someone who enabled me to experience myself differently and begin crashing through it. I've been almost compelled to keep working at it ever since. I was raised as a very high-achieving, productive, well-behaved, white Catholic boy—by my parents, church, and schooling. I have managed to turn around the focus of my achievement from outside to inside. I work daily at opening myself and loosening myself (a bioenergetics process) and freeing myself, getting more direct with people and taking more risks. But I do all this almost as compulsively as I used to work at performing externally. My goal now is to evolve to a point where I really let go and I'm really the way I would naturally be . . . not because I'm pushing myself, but because I'm simply responding appropriately and freely to whatever is happening around me.

SWEENEY: When a person discovers that a relationship in the past, or a faith of the past, has been destructive rather than constructive, I think there is always a danger that the emergence is going to be a self-definition based solely on rejecting the person who used to be.

VASCONCELLOS: Yes. And some of mine is, but I think it's getting clearer and purer as I go along. So I'm less reactive and more just my own simple expression of who I am. I'm sure now of my own life process and my own relationships and my own personal—mental, emotional, and bodily—processes. I don't think I'm often reactive or resentful now. There are still moments when I get in some really bad freaky places where I judge others and I hate the church and God, but those are increasingly rare.

SWEENEY: I'm personally happy that the object of your faith, the God that you've known, is blank. I think that's really—I'm using my own vocabulary—a great grace. And I don't know what's going to happen. You don't—who or what or why. But at least from the way you described it to me, to go from where you were in terms of your understanding and relationship with God to where you are is definitely an advance. Now the last question: Who are you to God?

VASCONCELLOS: I don't know. All I can tell you is that who I am is much more to anybody and everybody than ever before. I'm more present, I'm more responsive, I'm more authentic, and I'm more faithful (in the finest sense of that term, by anybody's definition) than ever before. And yet I'm still a long ways from where and who I want to be.

SWEENEY: A long ways from where you'd like to be. Is there something inside of you that is inviting you to this further development?

VASCONCELLOS: It seems to be, yeah. I suspect that's just the natural me, the life process. I find myself having an intellectual sense of faith about what I naturally, inherently would be and that leads me to keep working toward and risking being more open and loose and natural. And I have begun to experience my being, my body, pursuing some astounding, at times awesome, knowledgeable process towards my further liberation.

SWEENEY: If you were creating a faith or a relationship that you considered to be the most important, what would that relationship do? Or what would you want it to do?

VASCONCELLOS: For myself? I'd want that "faith" to be truly founded upon and nurturing of, a profound faith in the innocence of human nature and the wholeness of human potential. I'd want it not to require me to give myself up in the first place, and in the second place, to encourage me to take back all of who I am.

And for myself, I'd want a relationship based and operating upon just such a (mutual and reciprocal) faith. It would be unconditional, with a profound character of being present, of acceptance and of touching. "Unconditional" has become a very important word (and condition) for me. You know true love and loving are utterly unconditional. I want to be in relationships where I feel safe and trusted and free to let myself go, and to let go to myself. And I want to be present to other persons in the same way so they experience the same trust and acceptance. Only that is love. And therein freedom is truly experienced. Therein the person, each person, truly grows. And therein our capacity for loving truly emerges—in an incredibly beautiful and powerful way. Just incredibly beautiful and powerful!!! Isn't that what God's supposed to be all about?

WILLIAM SHOEMAKER

This soft speaking, shy person is one of the greatest jockeys in the history of racing.

SHOEMAKER: Who is God to me, is that the question you asked me? I must admit that I'm really not very religious. I do believe in God, but I don't really follow it as well as I probably should. I'm not into it like some people, but I believe in God and sometimes in my life I have asked him to help me when I thought I really needed it. That's happened to me many times, and I think he's helped me. I think he's been great to me. God's been good to me in my career. I've ridden twenty-five years and I've fallen a lot of times. I've been hurt and almost killed two or three times, and survived it all. I feel like he's trying to look out for me, you know, maybe more so than the average guy.

SWEENEY: Well, your professional sport is a very dangerous one—there are a lot of risks involved.

SHOEMAKER: I probably don't deserve it, but he's done it. I don't know why because I really haven't been that much of a follower.

SWEENEY: By a follower, you mean a churchgoer?

SHOEMAKER: I don't go to church. I do once in a while, but not very often. That's what I mean.

SWEENEY: Have there been any major changes in the way you feel about God now as opposed to the way you felt about God when you were very young?

SHOEMAKER: There's a difference. When I grew up in Texas, I was raised a Baptist. I think some of the things they did kind of turned me off a little. On Sunday saying they wern't supposed to dance, or drink—those kind of things—and as soon as they left

150

the church, they would do it, you know. That kind of turned me off religion.

SWEENEY: When did you become aware of the fact that God was more than just a religion or more than just these practices?

SHOEMAKER: I think the time that really impressed me was when the horse fell on me again, broke my pelvis in five places. I was really close to death, and I feel he saved me. For what reason, I don't know, but he did.

SWEENEY: How old were you?

SHOEMAKER: I was thirty-five. I was pretty old. But then again, as I say, I don't really follow anything. I just believe in God, and I try to do the right thing—be nice to people, don't do anything bad, help people when they need help—that sort of thing.

SWEENEY: How do you think God looks on you?

SHOEMAKER: He's been good to me. Maybe he thinks I'm just sort of a special kind of guy that he likes.

SWEENEY: If God were sitting down among his friends, how do you think he would describe you?

SHOEMAKER: Well, I hope he would say, "He's a nice man, he helps people, he tries to do the right thing, and I kind of like him."

SWEENEY: Has there been any experience in your life where you have seen or felt that God was really acting in behalf of another person, or person close to you?

SHOEMAKER: Hm . . . that's kind of difficult.

SWEENEY: Have you ever been in a situation where you wanted something for another person, and you prayed for it, and it was answered?

SHOEMAKER: I'm sure I have done that several times. I'm trying to think of one that could be mentioned here. . . . When my friend from New York had cancer in his eye—it was there for about two years—he came out here and I took him to the doctor. He had to have it operated on, and it was cancer. The doctor had to take out the whole lower eyelid, go all the way below the cheekbone to get all the cancer out. He took some cartilage from the inside of his nose, to make a lower eyelid for him. The operation went well, and my friend survived. That's one time I asked God to help.

SWEENEY: And he has vision in that eye?

SHOEMAKER: Yes.

SWEENEY: So the eye . . .

SHOEMAKER: Yes—he's all right. He got rid of all the cancer and everything. Had he gone another two or three months, the doctor said he would have been dead. It would have gone into his system.

SWEENEY: Is there a particular word that describes God better for you than any other word?

SHOEMAKER: I think he's very powerful. I really do. As far as I'm concerned. The things that I see happen at times in life—I think he's strong, good, powerful. He's everything that I would like to be in my life if I could.

EDWARD ANHALT

Winner of two Academy Awards, Edward Anhalt is one of the outstanding screenwriters alive today. His screenplays include: Becket, Maria Magdalena, QB VII, Man in the Glass Booth, and Green Ice.

ANHALT: Psychologically speaking, I don't distinguish between the *effect* of fantasy and the *effect* of reality; and I find the argument, if there is an argument, on the existence of "God" not important. The effect is important. So when I speak of God, I'm speaking self-consciously of a fantasy—not of what presumably is a reality.

SWEENEY: Can I ask how your dismissal of the concept of God as reality took place?

ANHALT: Well, along with many other propositions that I've heard in my life, which are made on a purely subjective basis with no evidence, I rejected it, as a little child. When I was first exposed to the concept, it seemed not establishable, and in itself absurd. Because to ascribe everything to one entity seems an absurd choice, a lazy approach to the situation—I'm speaking now of my thoughts as a four- or five-year-old child. Why not thirty entities? Or fifty? Or a hundred? The world is very complex. The universe is complex. Now the fact that most of the time it seems to have a clock-work-type mechanism—everything seems to be neatly arranged—does not imply to me that anything arranged it. And the idea that God arranged all these things, and that's the popular concept, the idea you get when you're first exposed to religion, just seems absurd.

As I said, why one? Why not a consortium of gods? As a child, that's what attracted me about the Greeks and the Romans. They

153

had many such entities. But there's no connection, no logical connection or scientific connection between what we can observe or what we can sense with instruments and this entity. There's the *effect* of believing in the entity which is observable. There's also the *effect* of believing in the sacredness of the king, or the importance of General Motors, or whatever. I believe that what we call the United States of America is as much of a fantasy as God. I don't think there is any such thing. There are people, there's land, there are factories, there's a bureaucracy—but a country—nonsense. There's no such thing, it's an abstract, a fantasy. Yet it affects people's lives. It makes war, collects taxes; people die for it; people love it or hate it. Because I personally think the country is a fantasy, my opinion does not invalidate the effect this fantasy has on people's lives.

SWEENEY: What about the concept of freedom? Do you consider that a fantasy?

ANHALT: Well, you'd have to define what it means. There are many kinds of freedom. Do you mean free will?

SWEENEY: For example, political freedom.

ANHALT: Well, it varies from country to country. There's clearly more political freedom in the United States than in the Soviet Union.

SWEENEY: Now, the reason I asked that is, a lot of people have died for "freedom," and my question is whether their death was for a fantasy, or whether it was for a reality. Whether it was prompted by a fantasy, an abstraction of a nonexistent "reality," or whether it was prompted by a perception of a reality that is not tangible.

ANHALT: Well, I think freedom with a capital F is a fantasy, but freedom of various kinds, qualified, observable—political freedom is observable in various forms in various countries—is not a fantasy. It's an observable reality; it can be recorded; it's susceptible to analysis. So people who die for freedom, you know, they die for whatever their concept of freedom was, or whatever they wanted—that seems to me a lot realer than God, or a lot realer than a country. I know that if we were in the Soviet Union now, this interview on the subject of God would be considered at the very least bizarre, and at the very most politically dangerous.

That's an absence of the kind of freedom that we have in the United States. So political freedom, observable freedom, is real.

SWEENEY: Up to the age of four or five, when you really took a hard look at the logicality of God, so to speak, did you have any other movements or feelings or attractions to God as "reality"?

ANHALT: Well, my first contact with God came through Sunday School books, where God was pictured as a, you know, an old Jewish gentleman with white hair and a white beard, roughly Michaelangelo's Moses. I was impressed to the point that when I saw the Moses at the church just outside the Vatican, I was really shaken by it, because suddenly there was the God of my four- and five-year-old mind. Anyway, I had been moved by that concept of God until I was about four or five, and what unmoved me was a traumatic experience, which I'll tell you about just as soon as I get some coffee. Do you want any?

SWEENEY: No thanks.

ANHALT: Anyway, you know the ritual at Passover in which the firstborn goes outside the door and he smears lamb's blood on the door, so that when the Angel of Death flies over, he knows that this is a Jewish household and a Jewish child, and therefore doesn't smite the firstborn—all this dating back to the Egyptians and the plagues?

SWEENEY: Yes, I'm aware of the ritual.

ANHALT: Well, our family observed it. Well, I must have been five, and I was the firstborn, and they sent me outside the house to smear blood on the door and wait for the Angel of Death. The house was near what is now the Bronx, but in those days it was just farmland—kind of wild. Now, at this point I really believed that the Angel of Death was going to fly over, and being a skeptic even then, I worried about his eyesight, his sense of who was Jewish or who wasn't. Would he get confused? I considered it a risky enterprise. And my mother didn't do very much good, because she said to me, "Well, there isn't really an Angel of Death, it's just part of the Passover." But I thought she was trying to reassure me. I really believed there was an Angel of Death.

So I went outside, and I remember there was a windstorm going on. In those days people had dovecotes—they raised pigeons. And while I was out there, the man in the next house released his pigeons. And there was this enormous flurry of wings—I was convinced that it was the Angel of Death, and my fears about him drove me hysterical. They had to call a doctor and stop the ceremony. It was terrible.

SWEENEY: Did they take you to the hospital?

ANHALT: No, they just called the doctor. So finally, after a great deal of head-shaking, and "strange child!," the ceremony began again, and then there was the explanation that it had been the pigeons from next door. Well, it destroyed me, because it proved to me that there wasn't an Angel of Death, it was just pigeons. And working backwards, I began to realize that everything that they were doing and everything I was hearing probably never happened. The Red Sea didn't part because seas don't part. And then I realized that if you're going to believe in plagues, if you're going to believe in the Red Sea, if you're going to believe in anything, you must believe in God. The Red Sea could not part without God, the plagues could not happen without God, the Angel of Death couldn't be there without God, nothing could be there without God. So, if there was no God, none of these things were true.

Now later on, as I got older, I realized that Jews were enslaved by the Egyptians, conceivably they got away at low tide, and maybe there was a swine flu epidemic or whatever. But then, I rejected the whole thing, and felt very put upon by it.

So, from then on, I was interested, but I never was moved again, having been tricked the first time. And when I took Hebrew lessons and was Bar Mitzvahed, it was meaningless to me. There was no emotion connected with it. And the only time I've ever experienced anything like the religious experience since then was at the death of John.

SWEENEY: John XXIII?

ANHALT: Yeah. I was there in St. Peter's Square when John died. And that was the only time I've had a sense of a presence, or an entity which was larger than the million people who were gathered in St. Peter's. And I got that from the emotional reaction of the people to the death of the pope, a reaction which occurred before his death was announced.

SWEENEY: Really?

ANHALT: Yes. About five minutes before. Spontaneously, everyone in St. Peter's fell to their knees, except a group of Orthodox
Jews, who were over in a corner praying with their prayer shawls
and didn't kneel because they don't. And it was very noisy. You
know, Italians're doing business all the time. I mean, the people
were selling things, and the hookers were working, and so forth.
And, it was the death watch—he died about seven-thirty in the
evening, just before dark, I think—and just before darkness set in,
for some reason, it was as though you turned the sound down.
Absolute silence. And everybody fell to their knees and you
couldn't hear anything. It was eerie. And while that was going on,
three or four minutes later the windows of the pope's apartment
opened, and the loudspeaker then said that the pope had died.
Now, that was a mystical experience to me, and that was the only
time that I had any of the feelings that one associates with God.
SWEENEY: If the effects of the fantasy about God have as much
power as the effects of a belief that is founded on the reality of
God, what difference does it make?
ANHALT: It doesn't.
SWEENEY: Okay. I can see from the point of view of logic, that
explaining a Cause that is nonobservable, nontangible, nonem-
pirical can lead a person to say, "I really don't know."
ANHALT: I'm saying more than that!
SWEENEY: I know . . .
ANHALT: I'm on the attack here. I'm saying stop bothering me
with all this because . . .
SWEENEY: Why?
ANHALT: . . . because you're all crazy. Because you're in the
position of a person who knocks on my door, and I say "come in,
have some coffee"; you sit down, and you say to me, "On the way
to your house I saw a creature eleven feet tall with fifteen feet
walking down the street." And I say, "Well, is it still there?" "Well,
no." "Did anyone else see it?" "No." "Well, then, how do you know
it's there?" "Well, I believe there's this creature walking down
your street." It's not a question of my denying the existence of the
creature; it's a matter of my calling a physician for you. Your
concept is berserk. You're confusing a reaction to someone else's
concept of it—your parents, or the church, or whatever—with

your own instinctive concept. You're reacting. If no one had mentioned God to you, the chances are you wouldn't have gotten around to it.

SWEENEY: So actually you're equating the real with what is observable.

ANHALT: Sensible. Not necessarily observable. Now there's a fine line there, because clearly—you asked about hysteria—hysteria, which may well be a weapon of God, can make you feel and see and sense all sorts of things. I don't believe that when I say reality and fantasy, the line is that carefully drawn. I believe that this is a fantasy because I see no evidence of the reality. On the other hand, I'm very confused about many things as to what's real and what's fantasy. I'm just telling you my reaction. From the very beginning, from the age of four or five, it was, "well, that's just silly."

But there's something else I want to discuss with you. I woke up in the middle of the night thinking about it—it has to do with the killing of Christ, that maybe he had it coming to him . . .

SWEENEY: I don't understand . . .

ANHALT: Well, I began to think of the actual killing of Christ, and I came up with this: The Jews who executed him, or arranged the execution, in anthropological terms, were killing the Minotaur. It's what the matador does when he kills the bull. It's the killing of the god. And you know, sometimes the eating of the god. They kill the god. They had the balls to kill the God, to crucify him. But having done it, they couldn't cope with it; it was too awful for them. So they became Christians, saying, "True, we killed the God, because that's the way God planned it." And in killing the God, because killing him or not, we believed in him, we are saved. They were unable to face the consequence of God-killing, which is a perfectly natural thing, it's like father-killing—every man on the death of his father is a little bit delighted. Anyway, that shafted me at four o'clock in the morning.

SWEENEY: So, in other words, to avoid the guilt they professed belief.

ANHALT: To avoid the guilt they invented Christianity. The Jews who didn't feel guilty stayed Jews. Maybe he had it coming to him. Meaning that it is in the tradition of the human experience to kill one's father and one's god.

SWEENEY: I understand all of that. But to conclude from that, that Jesus had it coming to him, I mean, it seems like you're switching from the action of the killers to the culpability of the one killed . . .

ANHALT: No, what I was saying was that God had it coming to him. I don't distinguish between God and Jesus; in the Catholic sense I "believe" in the Trinity. So I'm saying that God had it coming to him because he always has it coming to him. That's what he's there for—to be killed. The killing of the god, the killing of the Minotaur is growing up—the moment of shaking off the fantasy.

And if you watch serious bullfighting in Spain, you will see it in action. The thrill that goes through the crowd when the man kills the bull well is almost indescribable. I once said to Lou Miguel Dominguin, whom I was sitting next to at a fight, "You know what you're doing, don't you?" He said, "What do you mean?" I said, "That's God in there that he just killed. That's the power of life and death. You've taken the power of life and death away from God by killing him. By killing the bull, you symbolize man's independence from God." He crossed himself, with absolute horror.

I'm going to get some more coffee. You sure you won't have any?

SWEENEY: I'd really have to think about that, because there is the account in Genesis of Adam and Eve wanting the knowledge of good and evil. And in achieving that knowledge, they will become like God. The parallel here, it seems to me, is wanting to control the energy or the power, wanting to dominate the power of God. And how do you dominate the power of God? By killing it, or by eating the fruit that will make you like him. The only thing that isn't taken into account are the effects of dominating the power, dominating that bull. What are the effects of that? And in the case you're talking about—the killing of Christ—the effects were either a righteousness or an enormous sense of guilt . . .

ANHALT: Followed by rationalization.

SWEENEY: Right.

ANHALT: The concept of salvation through the death of the god is the rationalization of guilt.

SWEENEY: But going back to an example that you alluded to just a minute ago: What would be the effects of a man killing his father?

ANHALT: Well, I think he would feel the guilt that we all feel for an act of murder that we can't justify for ourselves.

SWEENEY: But would that be followed up by the kind of thing you just described, namely a belief in father as, you know, some supernatural being? There is where I . . .

ANHALT: Well, no, I think that the belief occurs before the murder. Why would you bother to kill God if you didn't believe in him? It's to free yourself from the power of God, to free yourself from death, really. Because God kills, and he makes life, but you don't, you forget that experience because you don't remember it. The making of your life is something you can't remember; you can see other people made, but it isn't the same thing. Your own death, however, is very visible and anticipatable. You can't anticipate being born. So. . . . No, I think you must believe in God *before* you kill him. They must have believed when they killed Christ that he was something more than a heretic, judging from what has been generated by the whole event, and I believe it was a kind of bullfight.

SWEENEY: Because at least the way Scripture talks about it, the reason that he was killed was precisely because he had claimed he was God. But what you're saying, basically, is that even the people who rejected his claim wouldn't have done it unless they felt or believed that there was some truth in it.

ANHALT: Yeah. I think that it was a marvelous opportunity to kill God, ritually, anyway.

SWEENEY: I don't know what to say to that. I'll have to think about it . . .

What about the fact that people sometimes have fantasies that captivate them much more than reality?

ANHALT: Well, fantasies are very creative. You get a sense of power from your fantasy, particularly if it has real effect. To believe in God—whump, there's your God; for most people it isn't even an act of faith, it's just a reaffirmation of what they've been told. To come to God, to have the experience that the Baptists have, or the Holy Rollers, is the discovery of God. Jimmy Carter said he was thrice born. That's a much more exciting idea than being Bar Mitzvahed at thirteen, confirmed at nine, ritually and comfortably. The ecstasy of God is creative. I've been to a Holy Roller meeting, I've been to a hysterical prayer meeting, and it certainly is very exciting. The discovery of God, real contact with God, including the fantasy of people who actually see Jesus walk into a room can be very exciting. But I get my kicks in other ways.

SWEENEY: Now, in your writing, when you begin with a concept, and you embody that in images built into scenes, you're constantly relying on your imaginative power, your power to fantasize. So—I'm not exactly sure what I'm stretching for here, but—

ANHALT: Well, if I were religiously inclined, I would have religious experiences somewhat similar, very creative religious experiences. Jimmy Carter obviously is very creative in that area, and he must get a big kick out of it. To be reborn in Christ at the age of thirty-seven must be a very heavy experience.

SWEENEY: The very thing that threw you into hysteria at five, the substance of the very thing, namely the fascination of the mind towards images, and power, is the very capacity that you constantly employ as a writer.

ANHALT: That's true.

SWEENEY: And yet you've rejected the one as being silly, and absurd, and the other you use as the basis of your writing.

ANHALT: Well, I use my imagination as the basis of my writing, my capacity to visualize, but I choose not to visualize what you choose to visualize. And I believe that most of the things that I visualize are susceptible to some earthly logic. I mean I visualize scenes of the Mafia in 1920, and they do things they never did, but they could have done. Your visualizations are very creative and imaginative visualizations. I mean, the whole concept of the Passion is . . . marvelous story-telling. I couldn't possibly aspire to it.

SWEENEY: And yet you did it in *The Man in the Glass Booth*.

ANHALT: Well, there's the use of the idea of salvation through sacrifice. I believe in salvation through sacrifice. The fact that the pivotal point in the story has no reality for me doesn't invalidate the effect. It doesn't matter whether I believe in "God" or "the Son" or "the Holy Spirit" at all. The picture would not be any better if I believed. Because what I'm dealing with are the effects of that belief in other people. And for all I know, in myself, as well. I mean I'm not impervious to emanations from the world around me.

SWEENEY: Right. I'm not even suggesting that. What I'm curious about is the fact that a great deal of your writing is based on your ability to imagine, to fantasize, and to create powerful images that are going to attract the imaginations of the audience. Why is it that you rejected this power—the Angel of Death incident—when you felt tricked by it, and yet you constantly employ it as a writer? Am I making—is that clear?

ANHALT: Yes, you make it very clear, because it's an enormously potent force. I just don't believe "God" is there, but I believe that man needs it to be there, or thinks he needs it to be there, or gets a big jazz out of it being there. In my case, I don't need it, but it's dope to me. And therefore, the effects of it are very measurable and very stimulating.

SWEENEY: Uh-huh. Now if I were a cynic, which I'm not, I would say that you are using the power that you were exposed to at a very young age, you are using that power and exposing other people to it.

ANHALT: It's possible. I mean, I am in no more real control of what I do than anybody else is, probably less. So you can hypothesize that, although I believe it's silly (i.e. "God"), I may in fact be serving it. Quite possibly. I mean, I've spent an inordinate amount of time dealing with religious subjects, and I've written several overtly religious films—*Maria Magdalena; The Thunder of the Sea,* which was about Lutheranism . . .

SWEENEY: *Becket.*

ANHALT: *Becket.* Yes, I have spent a lot of time with themes involving God. So I suppose I'm, in an unconscious or subconscious sense, not quite satisfied that I was tricked. In other words, the Angel of Death may very well have been there, but the whole episode was clouded by the appearance of the birds. So it's very likely unresolved.

SWEENEY: And this is perhaps your way of killing the Minotaur.

ANHALT: Perhaps so. If so, I'm right on, as the children say, because that's what you're supposed to do. Now whether I go so far as to . . .

SWEENEY: You're supposed to cross yourself now!

ANHALT: What if I go so far as to believe that by killing the Minotaur I am going to achieve salvation? But that step I haven't made yet. However, maybe, maybe God appreciates effective warriors. A person has to be at war with God. I'm sure that if the fantasy were to become real, the fantasy would want struggle. To believe automatically is too easy and very likely insincere. I think one should have to fight for belief.

SWEENEY: Definitely. Especially since your introduction into nonbelief was such a trauma. I can't conceive of your introduction into belief being any less a trauma. I suspect it would be magnified immensely, because then you were just a child, and your faculties and your perceptions were that of a child. Now you have . . .

ANHALT: Well, I got very close to Jimmy Carter's thrice born bit at the death of John. That was a profound experience for me. And so was the funeral. I think it had to do with John's superiority as a man, and the aura that surrounded him for whatever reason. In fact, once I watched him appear to bless the people, and I watched what in another time would be considered a miracle. It was raining—I have witnesses to this—and very few people were in St. Peter's because it was raining so hard. At noon the doors on the seventh floor opened, and he came—have you seen the pope bless the populace?

SWEENEY: Yes, I have.

ANHALT: And he came out, no microphone, and as the doors opened, a shaft of light like a ten kilowatt arc shot out of the sky, which was absolutely clouded over, and it came from a hole in the clouds. Like that! Within about a fifty-foot arc around the pope, and it stopped raining. Then he spoke and blessed the crowd, and while he was doing it birds came and flew around over him—sea gulls, *not* doves. He blessed everybody, withdrew, closed the door, the light went out, it started to rain again. (laughter)

SWEENEY: If you put that in a picture, they'd never believe it.

ANHALT: No, it happened, just like that.

SWEENEY: That's really amazing.

ANHALT: So we all went and had a couple of drinks. I mean, it was spooky. We even said, "You don't suppose that this is some theatrical device that they have here at the Vatican? You know, that they spring those birds—and where does the light come from?"

SWEENEY: Have you had any other "experiences" of what you would call God?

ANHALT: I've had some experiences which were drug-induced, experiences of great identity with God, and of God-given power. On dope I've flown through the air under my own power. I've experienced ecstasy. But totally induced by hallucinogens.

SWEENEY: What was that like?

ANHALT: Well, it was the experience of being God. I used to have it fairly regularly, on a combination of hash and absinthe, which can quickly bring you to God if you drink too much of it. George Antile died of it, unfortunately. I used to sit with George Antile at the corner of the Via Consentonio and the Alcala in Madrid—dope was legal then and so was absinthe—and we'd sit there, and smoke the hash and drink the absinthe, and regularly would extend our arms and fly down the street. And we would see all the people below, and inject ourselves into their lives, play our roles, and be God! Under this particular combination of dope we could manipulate everything, control the people on the street.

SWEENEY: Well, what did you end up doing?

ANHALT: I usually had sexual intercourse with most of the women on the Via Alcala. I had a rather sordid approach to religious experience, but I could have done other things. Today I would probably do more constructive things. My experience was sort of a Mary Hartman . . .

SWEENEY: So, apart from the experience at five years old and the drug-induced experiences, your exposure to God has been primarily through fantasies about him, and specifically through exploring the effects of fantasies about God?

ANHALT: Yes, although not a conscious exploration. It's just very heavy dramatic material. But it has not successfully pointed me toward a belief in the effectiveness of the fantasy. Now I would like to believe in the reality of God, but it's not an easy thing for me to do. I just can't do it. I would have to have some sort of revelation, some emotional experience, or some experience that would lead me to God. And I'm unable to have that experience, so I can't be led to God, because it would be insincere.

SWEENEY: If there is an obstruction to belief, I wonder if the obstruction is a logical one or an affective one?

ANHALT: I think the latter. I think it's an emotional obstruction, because certainly I have done and believed in many unreasonable things. So this would be a major step, but I'm sure that if I didn't have an emotional barrier I could make that step. But this doesn't make me particularly unhappy.

For a civilian, I spend an inordinate amount of time dealing with the question. And I'm able to go to services in Catholic churches without being sucked into believing in God. But I'm very leery about Hebrew services. I stay away from them because I find that I can be easily seduced. My earliest experiences were the Hebrew services, and I suppose I have a fear of being seduced again.

Several times, in Jerusalem, I was very shaky, almost losing control. I remember particularly one Hanukkah celebration, way up on a mountain, looking over the valley of Jerusalem, on a very clear, quiet night.

And another time the emanation was obviously moving in during the Stations of the Cross, under circumstances which certainly were not conducive to religious ecstasy, because while you're doing them, the peddlers are trying to sell you things. It's not a place where religious experience is easily attained. But going along with the religious tour and doing the Stations of the Cross was a very heavy thing for me. But it never really has got to me, has pushed me over the edge. And I would like to be pushed over the edge. Because I recognize the ecstasy of the experience, I would like to have it. But . . .

SWEENEY: Well, I really hope you have it.

ANHALT: Thank you. You'll be the first to know!

LAURIE KOKX

I met Laurie only once, and that briefly, in an art gallery. When she learned of the book I was working on, she wanted to share her reflections on God.

SWEENEY: What does God mean to you?

KOKX: The ultimate is nameless, indescribable, beyond telling. What is his name? "I am that I am," God said to Moses, i.e., I cannot be defined by words or ideas. As India's sacred writings say, it is the One "before whom words recoil" (Shankarachary, India, 800). Meister Eckhart said, "It is God's nature to be without a nature. To think of His goodness, or wisdom or His power is to hide the essence of Him, to obscure it with thoughts about Him. . . . Who is Jesus? He has no name." "I and the Father are one," John the Apostle tells us. . . . God is love, and love is a desire for something beautiful. Asking what is God? is the same as asking what is sea, wind, space, nature. Everything is related to and a part of; for it is the unity from which nothing can be separated that is God.

And what am I saying? I am using a lot of words to describe the indescribable, for how can words describe a subjective experience? How can words describe a wonder? For to experience God is to experience a reality beyond oneself.

"God," the word, is man's creation, and how can Logos describe the infinite? Though God is inherent in man, man has conferred upon him a mass of human frailties. God has become a personification of man, a composite of all man's latent fears and frustrations, a mass of contradictions like man is to himself.

One minute God is gentle and benevolent; next he is a cruel and insensitive tyrant. Man would rather seek a pre-packaged religion, one that relieves him of any "spiritual" responsibilities. For man's greatest fear is his own spiritual potential. Man would rather live vicariously through the beliefs, ideologies, and doctrines that history has handed down to him. But what has happened to man as an individual in relation to God? Man has allowed God to become the spiritual counterpart to the political dictator, a dictator that rules by fear, prejudice, and greed. With flowing beard and furrowed face the anthropomorphic nightmare dictates and interrupts the laws presented to him by man.

Believe in the Lord thy God and thou shalt be saved? Leave the thinking to God. What cowards are men, to leave the thinking to their imaginary God. Why was man given a mind? Why was he given a soul?

I remember in Dante's *Inferno* the circle of hopelessness, where all the virtuous pagans who were born without the light of Christ were sent.

No, this is not my God. God has given man the law of nature as the key to unlock the mystery of life. God has given man a mind to think with and the power to reason. And by viewing his own evolution, man is given the opportunity to experience life as a totality. For man evolves not only as a body but as a mind and as a soul.

Nature is governed by the law of opposites. This law, Yin-Yang, is the order of the universe. It is the basis of life and its evolution—darkness is to light; cold is to heat; male is to female; death is to life; moon is to sun; hate is to love; as evil is to good.

Man, from time primordial, has been instinctively aware of this law. Just look at the gods he has created.

A friend said to me once, "My inadequacy is that I don't believe in sin. For sin is the challenge to life."
SWEENEY: Hmm, interesting. I guess I look upon sin as a negation of life.
KOKX: Without sin man would never explore the reaches of his own psyche. He would never test the power of his God.

Nature is an integration of all life. And what is life but one continuous transformation? And when one realizes that all life, all the intricacies of nature, are actual mirrors of one's evolution, then one holds not only a tremendous respect but one realizes that each "specific element" of nature is an "aspect" of All.

Beauty is the eye from which man views his development. For beauty is the reflector, because the evolution within man is only equivalent to the evolution without. The universe within is only a mirror of that without, as Plotinus once said.

The soul cannot see beauty unless it first becomes beautiful itself, and every man must make himself beautiful and divine in order to attain the sight of beauty and divinity.

SWEENEY: What do you see as the finality or culmination of life?

KOKX: Life and death are one. Death is the nourishment of life; for life only progresses through death. Think of life as a montage of constantly changing shapes and forms, each making their entrances and exits, yet each overcoming, surpassing the other. Think of life as a spiral moving through the vast expanses of space. Think of the soul. What blasphemy to assert that God only manifests himself in the human soul! Think of the soul as the unknown factor that is constantly searching for the elusive substance that will unite it with all! As Eckhart said, "The core of God is also my core; and the core of my soul is the core of God's."

THEODORE HESBURGH

Father Hesburgh has been President of Notre Dame University since 1952. He is the recipient of more honorary degrees than anyone in history. (The late President Herbert Hoover had eighty-nine; Fr. Hesburgh has ninety-four.) His counsel has been sought on many educational, theological, and political issues.

SWEENEY: You can approach any one or all of the three questions, in any order you like. The questions are: Who is God to you? How has your relationship with God changed in your lifetime? And, who are you to God?

HESBURGH: The last one seems a little presumptuous on my part, but anyway, you want to start with the first one?

SWEENEY: Sure.

HESBURGH: I think for most people God seems to be rather distant at times, someone out there. As a theologian, of course, I've written a good deal about God, wrote a book on him once, but I'm not going to use all that on you. The most important thing for me is God revealing himself in Christ. The Incarnation somehow makes God a reality in so many different ways, but mainly through the life he lived, the words he spoke, the message he gave us, and the salvation he promised, especially eternal life. I think of him as the center of one's life, and this applies in a very special way if you happen to be a priest because you're trying to do the work of Christ. That makes it very personal to you each day as you offer the Sacrifice, as you take part in the prayer of the Church, the breviary. Constantly during the day the thought is there that if you're somehow partaking in the coming of his kingdom, you've got to be very much like him. Of course, we all fail a great deal and

I suppose we know God as much by how we fail him as how we honor and worship him.

I'm grateful when I read about Eastern religions and the great, indescribable something that becomes real for us in Christ—especially when I'm out in the Holy Land walking the ground he trod, looking at the places he saw, and somehow knowing that he is forever a reality on this earth. I'm always struck by what the Eastern theologians used to say about the fact that salvation took place the moment God became man, because nothing human could ever be strictly human again—this earth could never be the same again once he entered history. And that, of course, has been a very central thing in my life; without it I don't think my life would have much purpose.

So I guess that's the first reality that comes through when you say God. I think of him, of course, as God the Father. I think of him as God Incarnate, the Word becoming Flesh, and the total way the world was changed when he entered history. And the total orientation of our lives toward his kingdom and toward eternal life, which makes everything in this life, of course, fleeting and not all that important.

SWEENEY: Were there moments from experience in your life when that became really pronounced?

HESBURGH: Well, I think it was pronounced in many, many ways, especially when I made my final vows as a religious, to give my life to him. I suppose it was pronounced when I became a priest, particularly when I thought of being able to partake this closely in his work and offer his Sacrifice for the salvation of the whole world, which I've done meticulously every day, except one, for the last thirty-four years. Then I think, too, of the forgiving of sins and the spreading of his word, his message, trying to be like him insofar as anybody can.

God today is very real to me in a very special way in the Holy Spirit. If I had one devotion that stands out above all others, it would be the devotion to the Holy Spirit, that simple prayer, "Come Holy Spirit." In it you call on Christ for his promised spirit and you know that the wisdom of God, the strength of God, will be with you if you call on the Holy Spirit as God. God is in the world; we are not orphans. In the kind of life I live I face a lot of problems, and I have a lot of decisions to make. I call on the Spirit very often and I've never been left out, as far as the help goes.

I think God is also very real when in special moments of your life you see a great heroic virtue being practiced by some human being. I find God very real in all the beauty I see in the world with all its visual beauty, music, art. But more particularly, in human beings being beautiful, the way they, in a sense, incarnate the perfection we think of as God—by virtue of one kind or another, particularly in loving or standing up for each other, or giving of themselves totally for the good of others, or great acts of magnanimity.

SWEENEY: In terms of your life, what would you say are the major changes in your understanding and experience of God?

HESBURGH: Well, I think that as one gets older one thinks a little bit more of the words we say in the Mass every day about looking forward with joyous hope for the coming of the Lord, of needing him, of being closer to him in that way. I think the things I mentioned earlier about the sense of the Holy Spirit being with us all day until the end of the world, and telling us what to say and think and do—giving us the grace and help to do it—has become more and more a reality. I think the simple presence of grace in the world that one sees in so many ways in one's own life and the lives of others around us is powerful. I think as you get older you experience more of the tragedy and the acid of life, and that, too, is a way that makes one tend to fall back upon God. In times of great adversity, returning to God and hoping for his kingdom and salvation is very important.

SWEENEY: Is there anything in addition that you'd like to say about your understanding or experience of God?

HESBURGH: No, I'm grateful for the fact that we can find God in so many things in this world. When I was a youngster, of course, I was much seized by philosophy and theology. But the older one gets, the more one lives, the more experience one has of the totality of life, the more one realizes that knowledge of God and the sense of God is something that comes with the realities of life more than a lot of logical arguments. There are so many ways that God is found in life itself, in people, in beauty, in justice, in helping the poor. There are so many ways to find God. My mother told me her greatest reality of God was giving birth to a child.

TOM BRADLEY

It would be hard to even summarize the many respon-sibilities and duties of the Mayor of Los Angeles. Not knowing whether Mayor Bradley believed in God, and what effect, if any, it had on his work, I decided to ask for an interview.

BRADLEY: I suppose the best way to describe the sources of my faith in God would be to take a historical look at my life. I was born of sharecropper parents in Texas, came to Los Angeles when I was seven, and grew up in poverty. I lived in a divided home; my parents were separated and ultimately divorced, and my mother was the sole support of the family until my elder brother and I were able to earn money to help. With that kind of background, economic survival was burden enough. Add to that the cultural and other kinds of deprivation which a poor family suffers—and racial discrimination, which was very much abroad in the land throughout my earlier life, even to some extent today. When you are faced with these kinds of problems, with few concrete exam-ples of potential for success in life, you've got to have a source of faith to permit you to carry on. It was in this context that I've always felt that I could reach back for some strength beyond my own capabilities, and this strength was something spiritual, not something physical or concrete. It was, I guess, my early exposure to the church, the religious ethic that my mother implanted in me, that led me to reach for spiritual undergirding and support. I guess that's the best way that I can describe looking for, reaching for, some faith beyond that which is evident, some faith which is beyond myself.

SWEENEY: Was your faith ever threatened? Or did your faith ever advance, attaining new levels of growth and perception? For example, a lot of university students go through what is called "faith crisis," the time in which they step back from the faith that they inherited through the family or classroom structure and they criticize it very sharply. Part of it is reconstruction and part is just disillusionment.

BRADLEY: I went through the same process. And I think it was more a matter of disillusionment with the church and "church-goers," whether they were ministers or human beings who were part of my church experience. Being human they had their shortcomings, but through my disillusionment with them I began to back away from the church. It was at that point that I began to question teachings I had been brought up by, to examine whether or not the Supreme Being really existed. It was not a matter of losing total faith in God. But I frankly stopped attending church. It was a sharp departure from my prior total involvement in church activities. But this was a healthy kind of experience, a searching. And finally I think my faith was strengthened by it. This examination clearly reinforced for me the fact that there has to be some Supreme Being above and beyond myself and beyond other mortals. And it was in that context that I actually had a reinforcement of my faith in God.

SWEENEY: Some persons I have spoken with in regard to this book have talked about their identification of God with an institution, a church, or a form of conduct or morality. Others have really abandoned the idea of God as related to a church structure or code.

BRADLEY: That's right—because that definition is so difficult.

SWEENEY: Generally I ask two or three questions, but you have already hit all of those areas, and I don't know how your time is. Is there anything, in addition to what you've said, that you think would give the readers some sense of either your understanding or your experience of God?

BRADLEY: I guess I'd refer to a religious ethic which has been a guiding principle of my life: the Golden Rule. I strongly support a feeling of responsibility—you need to do unto others what you would have them do unto you. I try not to prejudge others. I try to place myself in another person's shoes and try to understand what it would be like if I were in that person's place. I think I gain thereby a sense of compassion, a sense of understanding and a balancing which enables me to deal fairly and justly with the other fellow.

SWEENEY: This Golden Rule—and also the contact with spirit, God, that you sometimes rely on—I would imagine is some source of comfort and strength, with the incredible amount of responsibilities you have. There are several people in the Christian tradition who had enormous responsibilities, and part of their own sustenance and strength came from some kind of interior attitude, or some principle, that they would return to, to draw sustenance and strength from. Is this principle, this Golden Rule, this faith, something that you feel is a strong right arm?

BRADLEY: Yes. As a matter of fact, very often people ask me how under certain pressure I remain calm, how I can appear to be rational and understanding, how I can be a mediating force between different factions. And it is that strength to which I turn that I think is the secret.

ERNEST C. MARTINEZ

I interviewed Ernie Martinez behind a bullet-proof glass plate on death row in San Quentin. His hands and feet were chained. I noticed a recent gash on his forehead. He's short, powerfully built, and has been in and out of San Quentin for the past twenty years. He told me he wasn't afraid of anything, even death. He is sentenced to be executed.

MARTINEZ: I was brought up Catholic. In my house, we went to church and everything. Communion, confessions, and all that. Then my father died an alcoholic and my mother remarried my stepdad. There was a time when my mother had to be both mother and father to us. And I took to the streets 'cause that's where the excitement was. My education came from the streets.

I got three kids. I never married the girls—never had time.

When I was eighteen, got hooked on heroin. I had a two hundred fifty dollar habit—had to have it every two days. It took the death sentence for me to realize how bad I had it and to get off the heroin. You know, I'm thirty-nine years old the fourteenth of November. I've been here the past twenty years, in and out of San Quentin. Prior to the state sentence, I did thirty months for "importation of narcotics." I did my time at Leavenworth, Kansas, the U.S. Penitentiary.

SWEENEY: Right here in San Quentin? The last twenty years?

MARTINEZ: Well, Folsom, too. I got out in 1969. . . . I stayed out five years. But I picked up another murder in 1970. I was acquitted. Armed robbery, kidnapping in 1971. Ended up in county jail after two trials, thirteen months. But I was acquitted. Stayed out for three years. Then I picked up two murders and a bank robbery where me and this security guard had a shootout. I was

176

moving away from the bank, looking back at the door. Like I told the people: "Don't come out. I'm going. I'm going to my car to get away." And this guard spots me. I didn't notice him. And without warning, without saying nothing, he took two shots at me. I turned around and looked, and he fires two more shots at me. Not in retaliation, more out of fear, I fired two shots at him. They both hit him in the chest, and he died.

In the other incident, I was robbing this Alpha Beta supermarket. And I had everything under control there, but one thing I forgot about was the liquor department that was attached to the market. The assistant manager was over there, and what happened is, he snuck up behind me and hit me over the head with a bottle. People, how come they try to be a hero? It's not like a holdup you see on television! See, I always blame myself as well. But I blamed that man right there—he shattered three lives by such a foolish move. He shattered my life. He shattered the life of the man who died, the manager, and his life, too, because I shot him three times, and he's crippled for the rest of his life. I'm on death row going to be executed.

There was a lot of publicity in Los Angeles about those murders. I value human life, you know, I respect human life. Like, sometimes I pray at night, you know? I say prayers for the people I shot, wonder whether they were in the doors of salvation, eternal life . . . or the bottomless pit. I've really given it a lot of thought. I wrote to their families asking them for their forgiveness. I tried to explain when I wrote to them. "Forgive me," I said, "because I can cope with any of the physical punishment here, but it's the discipline of the mind that's my punishment." I said, "Acceptance is the key—to accept all that's happening to me. Either I'll be executed or I'll stay here the rest of my life. I've accepted that. But don't think that because I'm under the death sentence I've got religion. That's not going to help me. I don't look at it like that. I don't care what's going to happen to me." But I wanted to be at peace, you know—here inside—I wanted them to forgive me.
SWEENEY: Did they write back?
MARTINEZ: Yeah. They told me that I deserved to die in the gas chamber, that I should be executed!

This whole thing has been hard on my mother. It always is on one's mother. The death sentence and all. Somewhere along the line in here on death row, I think I needed something to do with my life. I needed a goal, another chance to go back to God, to the Church. The forgiveness of dark things in my life, the salvation of my soul, where it shall dwell for all eternity.

Two weeks ago, my eighteen-year-old nephew was home on his first furlough from the Marines. He goes and visits his girlfriend at her house, and they were out front taking pictures. She wanted pictures of him, you know—he was all dressed up in his uniform and everything. Two nights before there was some kind of gang hassle. So all of a sudden these guys come out in broad daylight and just start shooting everyone on the block. They got him with a shotgun, blew his heart out, his lungs and pieces of his rib cage. He had a twenty-one gun salute at the Los Angeles National Cemetery, with a flag over his coffin—and taps. His Marine friends were the pallbearers.

That really hurt me, Father. I broke down. I wrote to my sister and said, "Why not me? If somebody had to go, why not me? My lifestyle calls for it. I've lived a hundred years in forty years—I've done everything from A to Z. Why somebody good who hasn't even lived?" Only eighteen years old. That really broke me up. It also made me realize how the relatives of those I killed must have felt.

I started being serious about the salvation of my soul, because I know the things I've done. I can't fool myself. I can't play mickey mouse games, because I feel that in this point in my life I've got to be honest with myself. I believe there is a God, and he might turn around and not be a merciful God if I were not sincere. I do not make a mockery of one's faith in his religion!

There's a Benedictine sister, Sr. Celeste Kamp, at St. Benedict's Convent, Minnesota. She writes to me, you know. And she keeps me on my toes with the Bible and my study of it. When she heard about my case, she felt sorry for me and wrote to me. I don't want pity, Father. I don't want nobody to feel sorry for me. I got that coming, you know. Anyway, Sr. Celeste and I are good friends now; she sent me a banner that says, "Be still and know that I am God." She also sent me a book on the shroud.

SWEENEY: The shroud?

MARTINEZ: She sent me a book on that. Fascinating. Really fascinating when I got into the whole book. And I read it from cover to cover. Then she sent me the picture that originates from the shroud that was left on the canvas as was the custom when burying the dead in those times.

SWEENEY: Oh, the Shroud of Turin.

MARTINEZ: And I stapled it to my banner. And I've got it there. And she tells me "never a fountain of sorrow." I won't say, Father, that I'm saved, that everything is all right. I don't say that, because there's times that I'm sitting there reading, thinking back, maybe tired, you know, from typing or something. And I'll be thinking about something, or maybe I'm thinking about what to write to this person or something like that. And I've got my banner hanging right there. I stop for a minute or two, and just stare at it in sincere fondness. The photograph, the story behind it never ceases to amaze me. Have you ever looked at it?

SWEENEY: No, I haven't.

MARTINEZ: I look at it, that face. I get up. And I say this to myself: I am nothing. Nothing. Nothing. But somehow he's with me. He's got something planned for me. I think that what's happened was to bring me closer to him. This was the only way he could stop me. This is the way I see it. I believe that this was his way of bringing me back to Him. I really believe that, Father. And so does Sr. Celeste.

One thing she did, she talked to me about praying to God. She told me all about that. She is a pillar of strength, a help to me in many ways. I wanted to thank her for believing in me when I didn't believe in myself!

I think you asked me, do you talk to God? Well, I turned around and got my pencil and I wrote this little story. I wrote what I felt and what it would be if God were sitting here and talking to me like a father. And me and him having a chat. And I wrote what I thought down. When I got done with it, it was four pages. I sent it to Sister Celeste. She got it and said it was the most beautiful thing anyone had ever written to her. May I send you a copy?

SWEENEY: Yes, please.

MARTINEZ: I just got a letter from Sr. Celeste two days ago, and she told me she was going to the hospital for some kind of treatment. So I have written a letter, sending a beautiful card, a get well card, and I'm getting all the men on the row to sign it.
SWEENEY: Great. She'll love it.
MARTINEZ: Yeah. I'll send you that prayer that she had printed in her community newspaper. It made me proud and happy that she thought enough of my composition, "A Verse in Prayer," to have it published.

> Look, God, I have never quite spoken to you before,
>   but my name is Ernest Chavez Martinez, and I
>   want to say, "How do you do."
> You see, God, I didn't believe for years you existed,
>   and like a fool, I never believed but this.
> I had come to be, within my heart, unneeding of
>   reprimand, fearful from the start of no beast, no
>   creature of this land.
> The realities I believed in were only what I saw
>   with my own eyes, no more than that!
> No one owned me; I was the ruler of my own poor
>   soul . . .
> But now the realness of all comes to me through
>   the life I've lived.
> In conclusion, I have dealt myself a sentence of
>   death to drown my sorrows in.
> Oh God, even as late as life might seem, I come to
>   realize that I indeed was my own greatest foe.
>   From the thirteen bars of steel that serve as the
>   front enclosure of my cell, today I looked to the
>   high barred small window and for a minute or
>   two in silence, I saw your sky.
> I thought of all the beauty I no longer can see but
>   only what my mind imagines.
> I stood motionless in realistic wonderment of all
>   your creation and I could only conclude I hadn't
>   really been calling a spade a spade. What I told
>   myself about you was a lie.

Yes, God, it is so obvious that I did my evilness
　　directly from the devil's workshop.
Does Satan boast how well I did or does he simply
　　laugh at me as I think he does?
But all this is very immaterial and of no concern no
　　matter what it might be.
But what is of great concern and the question in
　　mind from me to you is, will you stop to listen
　　to a man of my likes as I now talk to you?
I sincerely wonder, God, if you care to know me
　　better as I've already introduced myself, but will
　　you now shake this hand?
It is said you are merciful and just and that you
　　understand all that is in one's heart.
Funny under what circumstances I had to come to
　　this hellish sort of place!
Maybe it was to stop me from all the wrong I had
　　been doing to have the time I didn't give myself
　　out there to know you?
Somewhere I feel that though I can't see your face,
　　you very well see mine . . .
I say this because in the paths, the alleys, streets,
　　avenues, the roads I traveled that I have finally
　　been led here, God.
I feel you watched me all along the way! How
　　otherwise can it possibly be?
The Bible states you know the count of every hair
　　on our heads and the exact grains of sand.
I must then accept logically that I, but a mustard
　　seed among the mass of people, did not escape
　　in the shadows of the nights.
Yes, God, the darkness that worked so well as a
　　cover for my deeds, yet you saw!
Though the hardest and most powerful rainpour
　　and the darkest of clouds of day did not hide me
　　from your eyes either and in the darkness of all
　　this, you needed no light!

Well, God, you know the story of my life in whole,
   so what good that isn't there can I possibly add
   to it?
But it makes me feel glad I took time to have the
   pleasure of your company and that we especially
   met today.
I don't know the zero hour that I might depart
   from this surrounding, only you know the
   precise hour of that decision!
I'll try hard to not be afraid if you will from time to
   time drop in on me to see how it's going so I'll
   know the comfort of your presence is near me.
It's really been nice talking to you, God, and I want
   you to know I like you lots!
In the days to come, the courts, lawyers against
   lawyers shall fight the highest of judges for the
   space of judgment of whether I should live or
   die.
During the process of all this, God, I'll be here in
   the endless solitude of my cell awaiting!
I can cope with the days as I have so much learning
   to know much more of you, but do you think at
   night I can visit your house?
I know I wasn't a faithful servant of yours, and I
   knew you not nor was I friendly to you before.
But in sincerity, dear Lord, I look for my salvation
   and I wonder if you wait at your door when I
   come to talk about it.
Look, I'm crying. Me, Ernest, shedding tears!
I'll have to go now, God, but it's not goodbye, but
   just a so-long for a while.
Since I met you, I'm not afraid to die!
"Let not your heart be troubled; ye believe in God,
   believe also in me. . . ."
"In my Father's house are many mansions; if it were
   not so, I would have told you.
"I go to prepare a place for you. . . ."

RONDA CHERVIN

Wife, mother, philosophy professor, and author, Ronda Chervin is an introspective, intense woman with a lively, inquisitive mind.

SWEENEY: Who is God to you?

CHERVIN: God to me is if you put together everything great like Truth, Beauty, and Goodness, and you suddenly make it totally warm, you fill it with love, and it becomes a person, and that's God.

I was originally brought up as an atheist. Before I became a Catholic, I was in a suicidal, semi-suicidal state of despair. It had seemed to me that everything that seems good eventually dissolves into mediocrity. The feeling that relationships don't really last; they seem good and then they fall to bits—that kind of thing. There was no source of divine energy refreshing our basic situation; the world seemed to me very much like Sartre's *No Exit.*

I couldn't believe in God until I started to read about Christ. And I began to see how holy a person could be who was love. And I felt that the human race was too corrupt to have invented as pure a figure as Christ. So I began to believe in Christ as divine because of his uninventable holiness.

I never thought of God as an "idea" or "uncaused cause" or something like that. When I read those philosophical arguments they always left me completely cold. I felt those arguments really didn't matter. Because they were just ideas, rather than the God of love.

SWEENEY: How did you come to the conclusion that God was interested or cared about you?

CHERVIN: Well, the answer is strange—you won't believe this answer. I came to this conclusion reading Pope Pius XII's treatise on the Sacred Heart. Even though I basically thought of God as love and warmth, it wasn't that plain to me that it related to *me*. And the things I'd heard about the Sacred Heart seemed to do with something I didn't really understand. Then someone gave me this treatise. I don't like to read theology; but I wanted to understand this idea of the Sacred Heart. I figured that if I read about it on a devotional basis it would sound kind of yukky, but if I read something intellectual on it, maybe it would reach me. And that treatise . . . I don't know if you know it. It's a beautiful thing. There is such a feeling for what the depths of the Heart are. Most of my religious intuitions come from visual images rather than philosophical concepts. And Pius XII spoke about the physical symbol of Christ's Heart, how the symbol is meant to convey the notion that Jesus was a concrete, physical being whose love and pierced heart have become the source of salvation and life for the whole human race, and for me, personally. And after I read that, the sense of his personal love began to grow in me, through charismatic prayer more than anything.

SWEENEY: How long ago was that?

CHERVIN: Oh, ten, twelve years ago.

Later I read St. Gertrude's theory, *Meditations*. She's the medieval Benedictine mystic. Her *Meditations* are just permeated with a feminine spirituality, with a great sense of Christ being the lover rather than the savior with the love element secondary. And I began to realize that salvation *is* to be loved. Salvation isn't just to be taken away from misery or despair. As I said, my first feeling about God, and Christ, too, was an answer to despair, to existentialism. But it's a higher step altogether to see that salvation is love.

Before that, I used to imagine that experiencing Christ's love was something advanced mystics arrived at only in the "unitive way" after six hundred steps. Now it seems to me just a basic part of Christian life.

His love is present to me at all times, instead of being something I'd experience once a year at some retreat at a monastery. It's become so permanent that now I feel it's up to me if I want to relate to his love; *he's* always there. He is always loving me. And if I don't feel it, *I* create the obstacles.

SWEENEY: What are the obstacles?

CHERVIN: The feeling that what's negative in me is stronger than God's love. The feeling that I am incapable of being what he wants me to be, of communicating with him in the high, spiritual plane that such communication demands.

But lately I've found new aspects of his love. I find perhaps I don't have to transcend myself, purify myself, to be with him. I used to feel that in order to receive his love, I'd have to be on a tightrope clinging to him. But lately I've begun to realize that I shouldn't be on the tightrope; I should be walking right on the ground where everybody else is, holding his hand and walking along with him. He's right down here, with me. It's not me stretching up to him all the time. There's a kind of progressive realization that his love is not related to my best self, but related to me exactly as I am. The joy just in being, without always trying to transcend, to be purified. There's in me a tremendous self-lacerating drive to be perfect instead of having a humble, grateful attitude. But now I see this great healing going on in me; a being able to love Christ in the midst of the mess.

But then another obstacle arises. Knowing that Christ is related to me as an entire person, as an ordinary person, brings me another sort of pessimism! I get the sinking feeling that, even though he loves my best self and he's expanding it, still, the other part is so cruddy, it doesn't make any difference—I'm going to be dragged to hell by the cruddy part anyway. I guess you know what I mean 'cause you're laughing. But if I then go into conscious prayer, I realize that that's not so, that he loves me in the midst of my sinfulness. But in spite of that tremendous gift of being so aware of his love, I *can* get into that other pessimistic thing of saying, "Well, because he loves me so much and I'm still so horrible, I'll still be damned."

But as I said before, I never feel that God's love isn't there, that he doesn't love me. I just feel the failure is in me. Some people say there are horrible periods of dryness and dark nights of the soul. But I can't relate to that. I don't know . . . I really haven't figured out how they can feel that way. I know that for me, it seems to be up to me. If I want to dwell in his love, he's there. It's the present. It's a given.

SWEENEY: When you have your bad moments—your difficulty in communicating—what do you do, in terms of your faith, to come out of them?

CHERVIN: Well . . . in my darkest moments, when I feel unfit to live and consider myself unbearable and impossible, I just lie down on the floor and say, "Okay, I can't exist. So I'm not going to get up until you give me enough joy to go on." And he doesn't waste any time. Usually in five minutes' time I get a real deep feeling of peace and love, and then I start to move again. It's sort of surrendering, facing my emotions totally, and talking directly to God about it, instead of just stewing in my own frustrations and anxieties.

Brother Gregory said something that impresses me enormously: the reason Mary Magdalene is not sure it's Christ after the resurrection is because she's so hysterical with grief; and when we're hysterical, we can't see Christ. Then if we calm down a little bit we see him again, recognize him again. This is the pessimism I have; it has nothing to do with doubting whether God is love. Instead it's a refusal on my part to suffer, to rise to the challenge he sets for me. And I stew in my unworthiness, not able to realize that the cross *can* be carried, within his love. I just have to go deeper into his love to be able to do it. I feel that every time we're brought to a standstill, it's an invitation to go deeper; that we can't have union with him on the level that we're at now.

SWEENEY: Can you make any comment about how much of a difference the experience of God makes in your life?

CHERVIN: I would make a very extreme statement. I would kill myself immediately if I was convinced that God didn't exist. I just feel that the quicksand of evil would be so great that I could never pull myself out of it. I would feel that, instead of everything being saved in absolute goodness, instead of the good being ultimately swept up into God's goodness and transformed in the kingdom of love, it's all going to sink into . . . you know, that crazy song, "The worms crawl in, the worms crawl out. . . ."

JULIAN RITTER

I met Julian at an exhibition of his paintings. Although I am not an art critic, I could sense that the paintings done after 1970 possessed something vitally powerful and essential, as though his vision as an artist had gone through a kind of mystical transformation. I learned a short time later that his whole concept of God changed when he and two others were lost at sea during the summer of 1970, and went forty-nine days without food.

RITTER: Go on. Ask questions.

SWEENEY: Who is God to you?

RITTER: Who is God? I couldn't answer that. If a man can answer that, then he's a goddamn liar. If I look at my body, I say to myself, "It took billions of years to create that." By whom? By what? I couldn't answer that.

But even though I can't say what God is, I've got to believe. A person who hasn't got a belief, whether they call it God, or whatever they call it, must be naked.

SWEENEY: What is belief to you?

RITTER: To have a simple, calm relationship every day with nature. I pick up a piece of dirt and think it's beautiful. I pick up a bee, a flower, an ant, other beautiful things. And that's when I get that feeling—that I'm close to everything. That God is a part of nature, and nature is a part of God. Have you ever said to summer, "I want to put my arm around you"? Did you ever look at the hand and say, "Look, it took a billion years from nothing to be this. What is it?" You cannot explain why, but you get a funny feeling here, you see. It's a good feeling.

SWEENEY: Who are you in relationship to God? In relationship to this feeling that you sometimes contact?
RITTER: The closer I get to myself, the easier it is to contact God. I don't fully understand myself yet, so I can't tell you who God is. It's like digging a hole. You've gotta dig deep. And if you believe, there's always a guiding form—this sounds silly but it's not—a guiding form that will help you. It's beautiful to sin; it's fantastic to ask for forgiveness. The greatest thing is to know you are forgiven and then to sin all over again, till you overcome that mistake. And that takes time. Finally, you don't sin anymore and you find God.

Like drinking. You get soused. The first time you enjoy it. But the more experience you have, the more you realize that's a stupid thing to do. And then finally comes the clarity. It takes experience. You gotta catch the clap first. Then you've gotta be careful.

God can't do this for you. He can't reach you until you make contact with him first. It's like . . . if you hear some beautiful piece of music, you have to have contact with it. You personally have to have contact with the thing before that thing makes contact with you. You can sit on a bicycle—I never rode a bicycle—and say, "God, here I am, now pedal." But you've gotta pedal, not God. So finally you realize you have to pedal and it's amazing how beautiful things get. And if you fall on your ass, don't look up to him and complain. You keep on pedaling.

The longer I live, the more I learn and become a part of. Since God is all, and I'm part of him, I carry respect for that. It's just like when you are a young boy, you make love to a woman and you just dispose of the passion. When you get older, you want to possess; that's your ego. But when you get still older, you come to respect a relationship. And you understand that only in that kind of relationship are you in touch with yourself. You respect the beauty inside the person, and the beauty in the relaxation of the relationship.
SWEENEY: Some people have described God as energy, the energy that . . .
RITTER: I am very pleased you mentioned that. Each person throws out energy. You can walk down the street and feel each person throwing out energy. Also, each person throws out a color.

The energy is what you believe; the chances are, the pope has a most terrible energy. I can sit here, close my hands and throw off an energy so strong that when you walk by you fall on your nose.

We are controlled by energy, by good and by bad energy. I believe in it fanatically. Some person once said that each energy tries to reach its ultimate level, till it finally reaches the highest energy; and it is Christ, Buddha, and other great persons. I mean, there has been more than one Christ, let's face it. There's been more than one powerful man. And you reach this energy by overcoming faults and sins. You are born to overcome, to advance. If you don't overcome, you sink to a level of energy that's jealous and wants to destroy.

You gotta believe in energy, whether you believe in Christ, in a God, in a tree, in Buddha—as long as it's clean and good, it doesn't make a damn bit of difference. If you believe in it, whatever it is will come to your help.

I'm a fanatic believer in taking your energy and making contact with God's energy—like through prayer. Ninety-nine percent of people pray wrong. They say, "Dear Lord, my husband is a drunkard. Make him stop drinking." "Dear Lord, I need some money. I can't pay the bills." Or they go to church and they sit there, very artlessly; they stretch their hand out with a sad tear on the face and pray. That's not praying. Or they repeat a prayer that has so goddamn many lines that you have to be a genius to remember them. But real praying is just to say, "Dear Lord, I love you." Real praying is simply taking your energy and trying to make contact with God's energy.

Sometimes I just wake up in the morning and say, "I love you, God. Dammit, I love you. You take good care of me today." And I get a wonderful feeling within myself. I don't have to pray for hours and hours on my knees and go to church. I don't even have to know who I'm talking to, or know what that energy is. It's just instinctive, and it gives me a fine feeling. And I don't have to run around with Bible sheets.

I was born as a Catholic, and I rebelled against the Catholic Church when I had my First Communion and the priest said, "This is the holy bread." I said, "No, it was baked in a bakery." You see, the Church is false, it's hypocritical. It teaches you fear. Fear is a terrible thing. Man, the poor son of a bitch, all his life long everything is shoved down his throat—fear, bad, good. Name me any saint or any line in the Bible where someone said, "Go and sit under a tree and listen to the birds and pick up a leaf." Buddha was the exception. He said, "Live this life to the fullest, and if you do that, the next life is in front of you." Religion is beautiful. We all need it. But we need good religion. We need the good teaching of Christ. He is so misunderstood because the truth *cannot* be written down. You can only make men understand through demonstrations, through your actions and your state of being. The other person will see you and say, "How is it that you walk down the street every day smiling, and I'm miserable?" Then they ask you about your religion. You cannot go up to a man and say, "Look, you've got a dirty shirt on." But you can stand in front of him and show him your clean shirt. And eventually he will come to you and say, "How is it that you have a clean shirt and smell so good and I smell so dirty?" Then the man will accept spiritual guidance.

But instead, on television on Sunday you have God knows how many goddamn religions praising Jesus Christ and God, *telling* you you're a sinner and Jesus Christ will come and get you. They tell you to be afraid—you gotta get on your knees. Do they ever say, "Okay, go outside. Take your family and look at the beautiful flowers"? They cash in on the poor—the big fat Catholic priests and their diamond rings that could feed many people. They talk to satisfy their egos. You know, that's wrong.

Once I painted a bishop who talked all day long about religion. I wanted to say to him, "You poor son-of-a-bitch. Why don't you go into town? That woman needs a cup of coffee. That man needs a little encouragement. He's been drinking because he's lonely."

There are many, many priests who are saints. Yes, I've seen many of them. They get on their knees and help. But the majority, they're criminals. Go to Mexico, South America, to these little, little towns. Did you ever see the people crawling on their knees to Guadalupe for miles? And the priest just sits there, instead of saying, "Woman, you don't have to do it. God doesn't want you to do it. Just stay home and do a sincere prayer. Let me show you how to do it. Take a bath and use a little soap and water. You can serve God more than by crawling on your knees."

Listen to modern jazz music. To me, it is the most terrible sound. But let someone come in your house and play that on your piano very slowly. And it has such sad sounds. Every sound is crying for help. The younger generation is crying for help. They don't believe in parents because their parents are schlocks. They don't believe in the government because the government is greedy. That music is an expression of that younger generation. It's crying for help and it's sad. And there's no one there to help. No one. And not a single churchman is willing to help. They tell you to come to church and kneel there. Well, you see all the frustrated, neurotic, sexy women come in there. And you see all the men sitting there praying with the most holy-schmo face on themselves, and then when they go home they eat and then they go to their office to screw the other person by greed. And the priest won't help.

This is the most wonderful age we live in. The future is so fantastic because eventually man . . . I think he'll recognize the beauty that's around him. The priesthood should be the most beautiful profession nowadays.

There is so terribly much work to be done. But don't bring those thin Bible sheets. A pat on the shoulder, a pat on the ass sometime and a little food; it's amazing how much it can help. I remember when I was a kid in the old country, we had nothing to eat. And there was one Catholic priest. I loved him dearly. He collected—he got fired for it. His bishop said he couldn't do it. He got a little push cart. He put food on it. He put coals in it and everything. He pushed it all through the town. He said, "People need food first before they come to church." And the bishop came and said, "Gotta give them the Bible first. And then give them food." That priest was a good man.

Look at the paintings here. I paint nudes. There's no evil in a nude. Sure, I like to make love to a woman. It's my nature. Why not? But I respect them, see? A nude has colors as beautiful as fall. I have this crucifix hanging there. I call it "The Man on the Cross." I'll make a bet that sometime a churchman will come by and say,

"How do you dare to expose that man and show his private parts?" I'll make a bet someone will come around and say that's a sin.

Man should learn, should enjoy every bit of life. A priest should be married, should have a woman. I mean, don't be offended. How can a priest preach in a church, not knowing the warmth of a woman? Sex isn't evil. You go to Latin countries. They've got more bambinos around than anything else. What's the poor workingman going to do? Money he hasn't got. Food he hasn't got. What can he do? Lie in the arms of a woman. And then a woman gives children, children, children. But the priest comes and says, "Look, you shouldn't use preventives." If a priest were married and knew the warmth of a woman, he'd have greater understanding. Christ didn't say anywhere in the Bible, look, woman is evil. Only Peter and Paul mentioned it sometime that a woman is not kosher. I'm not trying to make an alibi, because if I get a chance to make love to a woman, I do. Only now with my stones and other things I have a hard time. But there's beauty in it.

If people would only recognize beauty. They tell you five thousand years ago God made the earth, and he got it together and said, "Let there be sun." But look at your body. Billions of years. What beauty, what thoughts, what energy is in it! It represents the progression from nothing to the highest form of development. And man takes it, declares war and kills, cuts throats, rapes. Man doesn't have a conception of what he's destroying, because nobody's there to teach him. Nobody's there to say, "Look, son, this flower here, don't step on that. Smell it. Stick your nose in it. But don't tear it up and put it in your pocket." There is much work to be done for a man who has a pure conception. These poor wandering souls have everything shoved down their throats but are never taught to recognize man. Go and look at the bars every evening, how they guzzle down their drinks to satisfy their vanity, their greed. It's sad.

Religion and the teaching of Christ are so beautiful if you read about them. The Bible is a fascinating book. If you want to find something to satisfy your screwed-up prejudices, the limitations of your mind, you can find it. But if you dig deeper and deeper there are some fantastic things in it. It was written by men who knew the weakness of man, and so they hid the truth like wrapping up a light bulb behind blankets. You've got to unwrap these blankets to get to the light.

I'm a believer. And I love my profession. And I love life. I love every little thing that Mother Nature has on this earth. But most of all, I believe in myself. I think all people must believe in themselves. It must be that each person has something deeper than a body, deeper than a heart, deeper than a soul. There's another X factor. You want to get close to that. It's your inner self; you can't describe it. But when you search within yourself you find everything else is outside. If you know your body, you understand only the chemical construction. But if you know yourself—which is almost impossible—you know the law of the universe. And if you know the law of the universe, you know that which makes the universe. Whether it's God, whether it's an energy. The unfortunate thing is that ninety-nine percent of people still think of God as an image of their own body. But if you believe that each cell in your body has a nucleus opposite and is just like a galaxy in the universe; and of this galaxy you have millions of cells in your body, and all these galaxies are controlled by your mind—and that mind is controlled by your own identity—you can realize that if you find that identity, you can become all. And if you become all, you become like a little grain on the beach. A little grain doesn't stick his hat on and say, "I'm the beach." It's part of the beach, and so he can't describe it. He is part of All—and All is part of him. No person could describe it. No person should. Because they will lock you up. They will crucify you. If Christ were on the street and started preaching, they would put him in jail for being the most super-duper hippie.

I have a Mexican worker, a very primitive, simple, person. He's the only one who looks at the flowers. He's the only one who really looks at my paintings. I have rich and powerful people coming by all the time. They say, "Isn't it pretty? You've got a lovely garden." Do you think anybody ever stoops down and looks at the flowers and smells them? The primitive Mexican does it. If there's a wilted leaf, he cuts it off. The other fellows throw cigarette butts in the garden. Did you ever sit in a house and a bee comes in? Kill it! Do you ever see a fellow take a bee when it's drowning in the water and take it out? I don't think you see people like that. A bee stings. It hurts. But nobody realizes that the bee also took billions of years to develop into a most beautiful thing that communicates. A stone has love, has a soul. Did you ever talk to a stone? It's nice. Try it. Did you ever talk with flowers?

SWEENEY: I've talked with nature, but not with specific elements of nature.

RITTER: Talk to a flower once. You water one flower, and pretty soon the flower will say thank you. There's a clock in nature. Then if you listen real close to the clock there's a flower back there that yells at you, "Come on, give me some water, too." Ever pat a tree trunk? I patted a tree trunk in Tahiti, and I looked up and said, "You're doing well up there, aren't you?" The fellow with me thought I was crazy.

Don't think that I'm trying to impress you that I'm good. On the contrary, I'm no good. I horse around. I screw around. I do all kinds of things. But at the same time I believe, see. And that's a helluva nice feeling, because if you believe in people and nature, it's just like loaning money. Somebody will return the debt after many years. Believing in the human race always pays you a reward. You don't have to scrape your knees bloody when you kneel. Just believe.

SWEENEY: What do you see as the finality or culmination of your life or death?

RITTER: I have a belief—it's just my own simple primitive belief. Heaven and hell are within you. I think my energy has to contact the other energy which becomes All. That energy in turn comes back to earth. I'm not separate. In other words, Joe, Jack, John Smartz up there are not all standing separately in a line. It becomes All into one since everything is All into one. There is no end, there's no beginning. Only man can think from a beginning to an end.

TERRY G. HASKIN

Terry is a gracious and warm person with a startling and refreshing sense of humor. Since 1973 she has been writing a novel trilogy: The first book was entitled Magenta Stone. The second is The Sapphire Tree.

HASKIN: God is 300 seagulls down here on East Beach facing north, and I drive up in my car with a loaf of stale bread from Safeway, and they come running over. They all have different sounds and different markings. And some of them seem to know me now. They come over and talk to me.

And God is in the strange little church near here when no one's there in middle of the day. I just go in and talk one to one. God is the nice part of me who tries to be kind instead of angry; it's like there's something, a little thing, that's nice in me. And that must be God. What the hell else could it be? I don't know. I choose to call it God when I'm kind and compassionate and understanding, when something or somebody isn't to my liking.

And God is very often a third party, like somebody else in a room, when two people are talking. There's a presence that's like a strange triangle, a trinity, a cozy little threesome of sorts. It's hard to put into words, but very often there.

I'm turning slightly into . . . would you say, a naturalist? I find that God is. . . . There's this mockingbird outside every morning who swoops down to greet me when I go for the newspaper at five minutes to six. There's endless chatter, and it means more to me than it used to mean. I don't know why that is. It just means more. Maybe it's not God. Maybe it's just middle age. God is Samuel Peats, the duck up the street who's really. . . . Well, I don't want to spend the whole hour talking about the duck, but I could.

But God is also—like last night—the wind. Last night there was the most tremendous wind storm. And I went out and stood on the lawn in the middle of it, and I just listened to the wind. When I was a little girl I used to do that, and listening to the wind, I felt a kind of mysterious presence in it. God is the sun rising in the morning. God is sitting at the Coral Casino and watching the tides, not only watching but listening. Mostly, God is a mystery.

It's like this marvelous, sophisticated head shrinker I first went to, Dr. Ross Moore. I asked him if he believed in God. We were talking about Hopi Indians and rain making. And he said, "Let me tell you. I was once coming back from Palm Springs in a terrible thunderstorm on a mountain, driving in my car, and I couldn't see. And I started whistling 'God will take care of me.' I reverted back totally to six years old." And I often feel that way; God will take care of me.

And he's my friend, Jesus. I don't know if this should go on record—they might put me away. But I literally do talk to Jesus. I always have, in my car, in my room, out in the garden. I used to not really talk to him so much as make a lot of requests: God make me better; God do this; God help me; God gimme. But you know, I went to Blessed Sacrament Church for a long time, and I used to go and light candles—having been Protestant I had never done that. And I often went over to the statue of Ignatius Loyola because it seemed the proper thing to do since it was a Jesuit church, and the Jesuits had been very good to me. And near the statue it said: "Give me only Thy love and grace and I won't ask for more," or words to that effect. And I used to think, "Oh, God, I need more than that. I really do. I mean I need the bills paid and I need to feel better and I need to make my place in the world and all these things." But I don't say that so much anymore. What does God mean to me? It means about that, that if I have his love and grace, I can manage.

I don't know if I have it, but I presume I do. I have it if I want it. I think that's how it goes. I once asked a Jesuit: "I won't be a Catholic unless you tell me that cats go to heaven." And he said, "Do you think they go to heaven?" And I said, "Yes." He said, "Okay, then they go to heaven."

And I think that what I think is how it is. See, like a lot of people don't, or think they don't, believe in God and heaven and all this stuff. Well, that's their privilege. Well, what you see is what you get, like Flip Wilson says. Right? Well, I choose to believe in God. I need to believe in God. So God is to me. God is a mystery. And he's Jesus Christ. And he's something that I don't understand too well called the Holy Spirit. That's what God is to me.

SWEENEY: How has your relationship with God changed over the years?

HASKIN: Well, it depends on . . . I mean if you want a chronological, sensible change, you ain't going to get it because my relationship has changed a great deal just depending on where my head was at. I mean, I've gone through all sorts of stages from being a very religious little girl from a very strict background where dancing was a no-no and almost everything was a no-no that was any fun, to an almost nonbeliever at the end of my teens. I became an agnostic for a while and became very worldly and socially conscious, bordering on Communism. And I had that kind of Mexican stand-off with the God of my childhood. So it changed during that period. But something occurs to me. That very simple sort of childlike thing that I did have in my very early youth has come back but in a more mature form. Only now, instead of saying what I learned as a child: "Now I lay me down to sleep. Jesus wants me for a sunbeam," I say, "Thy love and thy grace: with these I will be rich enough."

From the age of twenty to forty there were literally hundreds of changes, concepts of God to far-out, you name it: Eastern, the Dawn, Christian Science, all the metaphysical religions, Science of the Mind, Consciousness Raising, TM, ta ta ta dum. The trouble was some of it made a lot of sense, depending on what year it was and where my head was at. And I was always trying to come up and fit all the pieces of the jigsaw puzzle together and make a neat, tidy picture. One of the things that was so tidy was reincarnation. I mean, you know, that really made a helluva a lot of sense to me. But I don't need all that neatness and tidiness anymore. There seems to be a marvelous freedom in not knowing everything. It's like you can get surprised. I like surprises. Why in the hell do I have to know everything? I go back to the Book of Job

that I used to read to my grandmother when I was a girl. Didn't
God say to Job something like, "Shut up already. Can you make the
eagle fly? Can you make the mountains high?" You know, Job
asked, "Why? Why? Why?" And that's kind of how it is to me. I
don't know everything. And what's more, I don't have to. I don't
have to know. And maybe just that is knowing everything, the not
knowing, not having to know.

Somehow God has shown me the rule, taught me something
inside that is deeper than knowing. And at the end I figure I'll be
surprised. I'll be surprised! I figure it will all work out. So I've
changed. Or have I really gone back to *Go* on the Monopoly
board, where I started? What's the third question?

SWEENEY: Who are you to God?

HASKIN: Well, I must be somebody to God. A line comes to mind:
He who made you without you will not forsake you without you.
Who said that?

SWEENEY: I don't know.

HASKIN: What does that mean? God who made us . . . oh, hell,
that's getting into free will. I guess that I am here for a reason. God
is the reason for my being here. I presume that the biggest reason
for my being here as far as God is concerned is to—and this is a
kind of very tricky word, but I must use it—*influence.* Now that's
a very large, all-encompassing word, isn't it? But that's what it
means. I must be about the Lord's business. And the question
is . . . ?

SWEENEY: Who are you to God?

HASKIN: I'm his child, Santa's little helper, distributing cheer,
confusion, humor, and kookiness and spreading the crazy word as
I see it. I mean, you know, I'm not totally responsible for the way I
am. I sometimes say to God, "Why did you make me so crazy?
Why do I have such crazy thoughts? Why am I such an eccentric
and a nut?" And God says, "Well, someday you'll know. Just keep
doing your thing." That's what he tells me.

I have a favorite story about laughing one night with Jesus. I
saw Jesus and I made him laugh, and then I was very sorry. I said,
"Oh, Jesus, I'm not supposed to make you laugh." And he said,
"That's okay, Terry. You're one of my clowns. I have a lot of very
serious people down there. But I'm very short on clowns."

And I went around the world looking for paintings of Jesus laughing, and I never found any. There aren't any laughing. Isn't that too bad?

What else? What am I to God? I'm a comfort to him, and a laugh now and again. And he loves me. That was marvelous when I found out one time that God loved me. Really, I knew he loved me when I was six. Then I didn't think he loved me after, oh, for a long time. Years. And then I realized that God loved me. And I called up a friend of mine, Dave Barber, and I said, "Dear Jesus, David, do you know that God loves me? He just told me so." And I know he does. And really that's all I have to say about God, because I don't know much outside of that. I just know that I can't conceive of getting up in the morning and getting through the day, having to believe that God died. I think I'd die too. If God's dead, to hell with it all!

RICHARD CHAMBERLAIN

One of America's most highly acclaimed actors, Richard Chamberlain has starred in Shogun, The Thorn Birds, Centennial, Dr. Kildare, Hamlet, and numerous other productions for stage and screen.

SWEENEY: Who or what is God to you?

CHAMBERLAIN: I can give only my working definition or sense of the word God, a sense which is always in flux as my experience in life deepens.

God is the fierce Breath which precedes all creation, extravagantly powerful, infinitely tender. God is the whole kaboodle, the very essence of Being.

SWEENEY: How has your relationship with God changed in your life?

CHAMBERLAIN: My sense of God has changed considerably over the past few years. I'm less inclined to ascribe human qualities to God, to think of God as a remote Father, however benevolent. God is Truth, and Truth is not remote. Truth is life itself.

SWEENEY: Who are you to God?

CHAMBERLAIN: I'll try to state what I think we are to God.

Love is a state of being in which one is aware of the unity of all life. Our arduous journey from conscious separation from God toward love is necessary to God. Our growth serves God.

God is both conscious and unconscious. Each of us is, in a sense, an arm of God reaching toward a unique aspect of consciousness. Our growth, our expanding awareness, nourishes God.

Just as my hand is me, but not all of me, so are we God, but not all of God. As each of us awakens to our true nature, a tiny aspect of God awakens.

SUMMARY

The interviews in this book reveal a wide range of human experience relating to God. It is impossible to record all that I learned, and am still learning, from the many fascinating people who spoke about their faith and doubts. More than anything else, I feel gratitude for their openness, their willingness to share with me what is most often kept secret or reserved for only a select few. I also feel a deep respect for these people who had the courage to expose their faith to the public.

The value of this book, it seems to me, is the richness and variety of its characters and their convictions. In a way, the book is an encouragement not to fear "God differences" or discussion of them.

The strongest conclusions emerging from the book are that every person's experience of God is unique and that the greatest truths one learns about God are those woven out of the fabric of each individual's life. Another way of saying this is that each person's life will bring a special revelation of God. The fact that there was such a diversity of opinions concerning God seemed to stem precisely from the diversity of life experiences.

I was surprised at how litle mention was made of denominational or doctrinal differences, as though the formal and dogmatic divisions between religions were hardly a concern. In the same vein, none of the persons interviewed spoke of God as an issue of inter-religious debate, a fact I find interesting in light of the current institutional interests in ecumenism. The predominant attitude toward religious forms was that they were to be accepted or rejected on the basis of whether they led to an experience of God.

But among all these diverse and unique experiences of God, are there any that are common? Yes. The interviews give shape to a spectrum, which consists of three kinds of statements concerning God: *negative, positive,* and *unitive.*
• *The negative statements on God are those which negate God's existence, or state what God is not.*
• *The positive statements on God are those which affirm God's existence, or describe God's being.*
• *The unitive statements on God are those which express the union between God and the person.*
  The following are examples from the book of each of the three kinds of statements:

Negative Statements
Killing the concept of God is a form of growing up.
The whole concept of God is absurd.
The term *God* has no meaning at all.
God has no extension in the universe except in us.
God is not the one personified by man's good and evil tendencies.
God is not a person.
God is not an old man with a beard.
God is not controlled by ritual and self-lacerations.
God is not contacted through phony prayer or hypocritical religion.
God is not a task master or a judge.
God is not the property of one race or religion.

Positive Statements
God is the creator.
God is infinite Goodness, Beauty, Truth, Love.
God is the father of Jesus Christ.
God is Father, Son, Holy Spirit.
God is one.
God is many.
God is the created.
God is present in people, nature, beauty.
God is the force for good in people.
God is the source of peace, strength, courage, healing.

God is a friend, personal, loving, caring.
God is joyful, laughing, filled with exuberance.

Unitive Statements
We are the extension of God in this part of the universe.
We are a part of God.
We are three billion Christs in this world.
We are divine.
We are becoming God.
We are God.

This spectrum indicates a range of human statements and experiences of God from atheism to divine identity. It is not my place to prove which of the statements are more true. My purpose in this book has been to listen and observe. Personal exposure to this spectrum has been a profound source of understanding and consolation to me.

From a psychological point of view, I was both comforted and fascinated by even the atheistic statements on God, because they were consistent with a shocking or negative experience relating to God. This consistency of God-statements flowing from lived experiences was a common factor in the interviews.

A few of the people interviewed had experienced all the stages of the spectrum; some, only aspects of one of the stages. The overwhelming conclusion from the sum of the interviews is that God, or the One people refer to as God, is very much a part of human experience and consciousness.

EPILOGUE

It's Christmas night, late. I tried to write this Epilogue several weeks ago, but couldn't. A woman had called me to tell me that three years ago she had encouraged her twenty-one-year-old daughter to testify in court about a murder she had witnessed. Her daughter, she said, mentioned how frightened she was to do this. Three months after she testified she was murdered.

The woman began crying over the phone: "I hated God for that. I hated myself. I cursed him. All my daughter was trying to do was what's right. Why did he let that happen, Father? Why?"

Today I felt the bitterness of another mother, a devout life-long Catholic and friend. She is refusing to go to Mass this day, Christmas, because three nights ago her daughter committed suicide.

And so the anger and bitterness toward God, the hatred, no matter how lasting or fleeting, is an experience felt by others, perhaps many others. Thus I feel an urgency to say something to them and to anyone whose suffering leads them to doubt "God": *You are not alone.*

Pain, resentment, confusion, rage—when these become excruciatingly intense, we seem to flounder on the very brink of life and death. I have now buried so many people that I am certain of this: when a loved one dies, there is frequently a kind of psychological death borne by those left behind. It is at these crucifying moments of loss that faith and love seem to war with one another.

The Christian faith I was raised in asserts that sacrifice and death motivated by love lead to fullness of life, even beyond death. This faith, at its deepest psychological roots, tries to assure us that our ultimate beginning and end is God—not sickness or health, wealth or destitution, life or death, husband, wife, father, mother, son or daughter, brother or sister, or friend. The whole dynamic of Christian faith seems to be to *entrust,* to hand over to "God in Christ" birth, life, love, suffering, divorce, death, and chaos.

But the whole dynamic of love is to *embrace,* to be one with the beloved in birth, life, suffering, separation, and even death. Love tells us that the one thing precious above all else is union, presence, mutual being with and acceptance of all that the other and I are together. Love, it seems to me, is the intimate and the daily choices leading to this oneness.

Death divorces us from this oneness, while faith challenges us—at the moment when we are most crippled—that our beloved belongs to God. Death ushers in that chasm of separation, of uncertainty and darkness that leaves us bereft of the one who has brought us to life through love. Thus the cry, the anguish, the raging against God—because the one whose life has brought us love is dead, because our faith has told us that God is good, God is love. And yet, the one who is good, who is love and life to us, has been snatched up in death, either by the will or by the acquiescence of God. How can God, who is love, separate us from the one who is love to us? How can God will or tolerate this most cruel and exacting torment: to create and encourage us to love, and at the same time expect us to accept "in faith" that horrible reality that steals away our love?

Death can cause faith and love to be enemies.

This conflict can be transformed into a new wisdom and harmony when love is bonded not only to flesh and blood and spirit of the ones we love on this earth but also to flesh and blood and spirit of all that was, is, and shall be—on this earth or transcending it.

Personally, I have not yet been granted this level of faith or love. I am still in anguish over human suffering and death. The anger and rage I felt ten years ago have gone and seem to have been replaced by a tone of awareness, a sorrow I feel every time I sense someone else struggling with God and death. This, it seems to me, is the great trial Jesus asked us to pray about in the Our Father—". . . and lead us not into temptation . . ."—the temptation to equate death with evil, the temptation to say that death and God are irreconcilable, the temptation to feel that death and love are mutually exclusive, the temptation to feel that death can destroy faith and love and God. Ten years ago, when faced with this temptation, I gave in to it. I ended up hating myself, God, and life, and thus became a form of living death.

Someday, I hope to more fully understand the people and events that gradually brought me out of this darkness. The care and love of friends prevented total despair. The many persons interviewed in this book were a profound help, because I felt I was not alone in questioning God. Celebrating Mass with handicapped children resurrected in me the possibility of faith. Burying Chicano gang members demonstrated the hard reality that loyalty to family and neighborhood are, for some, more valuable than life or death.

Who is God to me? Sometimes silence; sometimes a quiet pain; sometimes others who are plunging into this darkness; sometimes birth—birth of a smile, a gesture of love. I don't know who God is to me, but something of grace has happened since the explosion of hatred and anger several years ago. Because I find myself wanting to know, because I find myself seeking again, wanting to breathe, to smile, to bring the broken and still healing beginnings of love to a world and a God I hope will embrace me in a much deeper faith if I am to be crushed again.